# Looking for the Roses

D1738454

E. Charlese Spencer

**Looking for the Roses**

Published by Iceni Books™.

610 East Delano Street, Suite 104, Tucson, Arizona 85705, U.S.A.
www.icenibooks.com

ISBN: 1-58736-553-7
LCCN: 2005909430

This book is dedicated to the loving memory of my nephew, KEVIN SPENCER LYNCH, who quickly learned to play any musical instrument available or made one! At the age of nineteen, he could not be persuaded that he was handsome, intelligent, talented, useful, and loved by everyone who knew him.

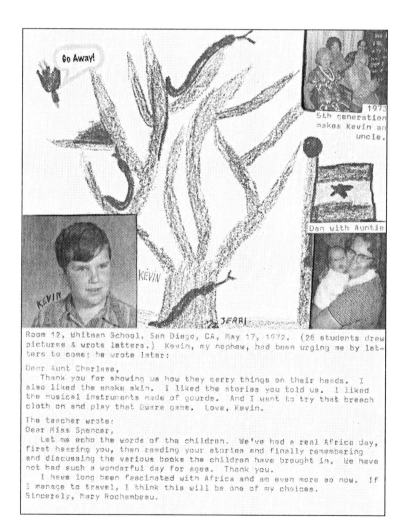

Room 12, Whitman School, San Diego, CA, May 17, 1972. (26 students drew pictures & wrote letters.) Kevin, my nephew, had been urging me by letters to come; he wrote later:

Dear Aunt Charlese,
    Thank you for showing us how they carry things on their heads. I also liked the snake skin. I liked the stories you told us. I liked the musical instruments made of gourds. And I want to try that breech cloth on and play that Oware game. Love, Kevin.

The teacher wrote:
Dear Miss Spencer,
    Let me echo the words of the children. We've had a real Africa day, first hearing you, then reading your stories and finally remembering and discussing the various books the children have brought in. We have not had such a wonderful day for ages. Thank you.
    I have long been fascinated with Africa and am even more so now. If I manage to travel, I think this will be one of my choices.
Sincerely, Mary Rochambeau.

# ACKNOWLEDGEMENTS

MOST OF MY FAMILY history came from Mom and Dad; they saved items from their parents. Dad's cousin, Alma Joy, added data about the family of my Grandmother Sarah Adkins Spencer. Mom's cousin, Lorena, did the same for the Cox family. I learned a lot on a trip to Plains, Texas, with Aunt Leonora. We visited the local court house and daughters of the Luna family. (See Photos)

# TABLE OF CONTENTS

# PREFACE

July 1996 Mountainair, New Mexico. Rev. and Mrs. H. Milt Fulfer, NMDC Superintendent 1940-1952. His wife, Rose, wrote:

"Charlese, Milt cannot see to write any more. He said for you to write about the things we discussed on the phone. Mail it to us and he can sign it."

Our nostalgic phone call went something like this, "I knew your parents for many years before your whole family accepted Christ in 1937. I became NMDC Superintendent in 1940 (at Amarillo, Texas) when the Texaco District Split into New Mexico and West Texas Districts. A. C. Bates had been superintendent before that; he and his family knew the Spencer family. From the time I set the T or C (Hot Springs) church in order, I have known of your dedication to God and your work in the state. We followed your progress as you graduated from Southwestern Bible College, held revivals, and pastored three churches: Dora, Dexter, and Grants. We knew when you took your nurses training while attending First Assembly in Albuquerque. We observed your progress as a missionary and nurse-midwife in Africa. We are anxiously awaiting your book.

*While every New Mexico superintendent was alive when I started my book, most have gone to their rewards; it is so of Rev. Milt Fulfer.*

# Times of My Life

# FOREWORD

September 1996, Portales, New Mexico. Rev. and Mrs. Earl G. Vanzant, NMDC Superintendent 1968-1981.

"In every age God has had witnesses to speak for Him," so stated Noel Perkin, a great missionary leader of the Assemblies of God. Charlese Spencer was chosen of God to be one of His witnesses in Africa.

Early in life Charlese showed her love for Christ through her service for Him. While still in high school, she taught Sunday school classes and served as a leader of church youth groups.

A scripture that characterized her was Proverbs 3:6— "In all thy ways acknowledge him, and he shall direct thy paths." She followed the Lord's leading to enroll at SBI (now Southwestern Assemblies of God University). While a student there, she felt God calling her into the ministry.

Assisting in revivals in New Mexico prepared her to fill the call to missions in Africa. When she visited the church I was pastoring in Portales, New Mexico, my wife and I were impressed with the sense of her call to missions. Although she received official endorsement as an Assemblies of God missionary, she asked for my personal endorsement and approval as a minister and presbyter in her going to Africa as a missionary. I gave my whole-hearted approval.

Our confidence in her was shown by financial support given by our church. Later, I would have the opportunity to

9

help raise money at district meetings for needs she reported. One unique need for Africa was money to buy building materials, such as cement and metal roofing. She insisted she would mix concrete and put roofs on buildings if we would supply the money—and she did!

Charlese served as a nurse practitioner, teacher of the gospel, and a builder of facilities. Her love for her Lord and her love for the people was so clear. She paid a high personal price but did not waiver. What a great witness she left to the people of New Mexico and Africa.

(With thanks to my son, Thurman Vanzant, for wording and typing.) Signed: Earl G. Vanzant.

*I regret that Rev. and Mrs. Vanzant departed this life before they read my book.*

# INTRODUCTION

PEOPLE IN AFRICA AND America are urging me to tell my story. My childhood had a lot of the unusual, as I grew up in the "American wild, wild, west." It prepared me for West Africa. Americans and others are just now discovering both and seem to like what they have found! Readers may laugh, cry, agree, disagree, be surprised, or even be shocked! So, fact or fiction, this is how I remember it.

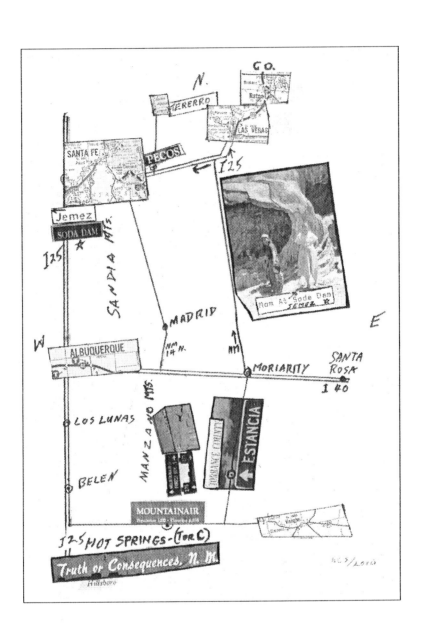

CO.

N.

TIERERRO

Raton

LAS VEGAS

SANTA FE

PECOS

I 25

Jemez

SODA DAM

I 25

SANDIA MTS.

Mom At Soda Dam
JEMEZ

MADRID

E

W

ALBUQUERQUE

Nm
14 N.

Nm

MORIARITY

SANTA ROSA

I 40

LOS LUNAS

MANZANO MTS.

TORRANCE COUNTY

ESTANCIA

BELEN

MOUNTAINAIR

Vaugn

I 25 HOT SPRINGS - (Tor C)

Truth or Consequences, N. M.

Hillsboro

# CHAPTER 1

## *My Spencer-Adkins Roots*

## My Grandfather, B. B. Spencer

WE STOOD IN A mass of humanity. The swirling dust stuck to our sweaty bodies. In Medicine Lodge, Kansas, the wagons swung into a tight circle. Mounted Indians with spears, bows, and arrows circled the wagons. Their cries were deafening. I, Elsie Charlese Spencer, was busy rolling a 16 mm movie camera. It was 1967.

We were Wesley School of Nursing teachers and a friend, Betty Olsen, all from Wichita. We came to observe a pageant of the arrival of the wagon trains in the 1870s. Ilsa Steg, director of the Wesley Nursing Program, was with us. She had immigrated to America from Germany as a child with her parents; she was one proud American! Since hiring me in 1966, she had worked hard to show me the points of interests in Kansas so I would remain as obstetrics instructor. This had included a visit to a registered Charolais cattle ranch and now the wagon trains. I had previously spent six years in West Africa as a nurse practitioner and midwife and was thinking of going back there.

"Miss Steg," I said, "I am going to show this film in Africa as an area where we recruit our student nurses." She shrieked, "I'll haunt you to your grave!" We laughed. I told her that around 1873, my grandfather, Ben Spencer, then an unmarried teenager, and his mother most certainly were driving two of those wagons. (Ilsa Steg died of cancer soon after I left Kansas.)

Benjamin Boyd Spencer, my grandfather, was born on Christmas Day, 1854. How far he would wander from his birthplace of Louis Center, Ohio. How far I, his granddaughter, would roam from New Mexico where I was born. I arrived in West Africa October 1954, one hundred years after his birth. Ben Spencer and Elizabeth, his mother, lived on their farm in Illinois after the death of his father. Restlessness seemed to cause their journey far west to Dodge City, Kansas. Ben, still a teenager, hunted buffalo along with many other men. He worked at shipping hides of cattle and buffalo east to Chicago. In the 1870s at Medicine Lodge, Kansas, Ben learned the sawmill trade. The railroads were moving west and needed crossties. Almost one hundred years had brought me, his granddaughter, full circle to Kansas in the 1970s to watch the pageant of his arrival west.

Young Ben followed the sawmill trade to Oklahoma Territory, where he bought a sawmill. He met and married Ida, his first wife; she was part Cherokee. In 1880, Ben and Ida brought a wagon train from Oklahoma Territory to White Oaks, New Mexico Territory. Jim, their first child, was born on that journey; Maude and Mary were born later. Ben's mother, Elizabeth, was a hardy pioneer woman who drove her own wagon. One wagon in the long train carried the sawmill. Four yoke of oxen pulled the thirty-foot, three-ton, steam boiler to provide power for the sawmill. Such a feat through rocky hills and canyons, over sand and rivers! White Oaks, near Alamogordo, needed lumber for houses because of a gold rush. Crossties were needed for railroad tracks from New Mexico's eastern border to White Oaks and south to El Paso, Texas. Ida's sister and husband, the Pete Hauts, were on that wagon train from Oklahoma. My father spoke amiably of Pete Haut, whom he knew as a child. As late as 1968 in Pason, Arizona, my Aunt Leonora took me to visit Walter Haut, Pete's son. Walter told me, "Your Grandfather Ben Spencer was a powerful wagon boss." He showed me pictures of his mother and his Aunt Ida, Ben's first wife; they were beautiful women.

For my aging father, Charles's, birthdays in later years, I took him on short trips. We went to places where his father, Ben, had lived or our immediate family had lived while I was growing up, and there were many of them. In June 1988 when Dad was eighty-seven, we drove to White Oaks. We located a Western bar-museum, went in, and asked, "Has anyone heard of Ben Spencer?" A near picture-perfect Hispanic gentleman, with apparently no teeth, came suddenly alert from a doze. "Ah, si, si! You mean Ben Spencer who moved to the Manzano Mountains?" My dad's Spanish was rusty in his later years, but between his partial Spanish and the other man's partial English, we learned that the location of Ben's sawmill in 1880 was now private property. The man directed us down unpaved roads, but we found only fences with no gates.

In 1887 Ben ox-carted the huge boiler from White Oaks to the Manzano Mountains. First, he set up his sawmill at Barranca Canyon, and then in several places along the eastern slopes. There was no official money in New Mexico Territory to pay his nearly one hundred employees. He had his money minted into coins of twenty-five cents, fifty cents, and one dollar by a company in the East, who shipped it to Albuquerque by Wells Fargo. He paid workers daily in coins and had a commissary where they could buy staples: bulk pinto beans, chili peppers, salt pork, Arbuckle Coffee, cotton yard goods, harness for horses, hinges, nails, sticks of peppermint candy in tinfoil and basic medicines. There were no doctors; Ben even helped local pregnant women in trouble at delivery time.

At some point, Ben and Ida divorced, and she married

a local man, a Mr. Munsey, who worked for Ben. Since Ida
was the mother of Ben's three older children, she was often
a guest in his home on holidays. Ben married a second wife;
she was from the East. For health reasons, she returned to
Ohio to deliver their one son, Boyd. She died, and her parents raised Boyd. Boyd visited his dad in New Mexico and
joined the U.S. Army in World War I. Sarah, my grandmother, was Ben's third wife. They had four boys, Floyd, born
at Escabosa, and Charles, John, and Roy, born at East View.
Ben's mother, Elizabeth, lived in his home during all three
marriages. She filed for her own New Mexico land across the
road from Ben's at East View. She died at age eighty-three in
1905 and is buried at Eastview. (On newer maps East View
is one word.)

Estancia Valley was sheep and cattle country. The Manzano foothills, including the Mountainair area, had booming pinto bean farms. Lumber was needed for housing. Ben
sold lumber in Estancia, the county seat, to Gross Kelley in
Albuquerque and John Becker in Belen. Gross Kelley owned
many acres of land in the Manzanos. They paid sixteen dollars per one thousand board feet of lumber from their own
trees, felled, sawed, and delivered to them in Albuquerque.

To obtain contracts for lumber orders, Ben and a friend,
Willie Dow of Chilili, traveled the areas in a fast buggy pulled
by Ben's matched team. One horse was a light bay called
Chief, and the other horse was called Blue. To fill those orders, they drove fleets of up to twenty huge wagonloads of
the heavy lumber. The trail led them over the rugged Manzano Mountains along the route later known as Highway 14,
and now called Highway 337 South in the Tijeras Canyon.
That journey took them through box canyons where heavy
loads sunk into sandy arroyo beds. They watched for flash
floods that could wash them down the canyon. Today, even
with paved roads, that route can be winding and treacherous—and beautiful.

In 1900, Ben had a sawmill near Escabosa; his mailing address was Chilili. Through the years, the young people of the mountain villages competed in baseball and other sports. Even small towns like Abo and Hillsboro had racetracks, and Ben Spencer and Willie Dow owned racehorses. Ben bought his racehorses at the Jim Newman Quarter Horse Ranch, in Sweetwater, Texas. One was a dark bay called Prince. Modock, a stallion Ben owned, never lost a race. The Vallejo family, possibly from Mexico, owned a racehorse called Paleto Secco (dry shoulder). When Modock was matched to race him, people bet cows, guitars, fiddles, and money. Jim, Ben's first son, rode Modock and won over Paleto Secco by sixty feet in a quarter-mile race. In later years, Charles, my father, rode Modock.

When Ben's horses or Hereford cattle were rustled, he collected a group of riders and made a trip to the Ladron (thief) Mountain, south of Belen and west of the Rio Grande. He found his branded animals and took them home. His sons say, "He was never without his gun; he even strapped it on when he went to the outhouse." Inside the house, he paced the floor with his hands behind him, flipping the long tails of his overcoat; he was a restless man. From 1900 to 1908, the railroad tracks for the Belen cutoff were being laid from Willard to Mountainair and on through Abo Pass to Belen. Lumber was needed for crossties and trestles. Ben Spencer's lumber can still be found in bridges that span the canyons.

The town of Mountainair was incorporated in 1903. Officers appointed were E. S. Stover, president; B. B. Spencer, vice president and treasurer; Col. E. C. Manning, secretary and general manager. G. V. Hanlon, J. W. Corbett, and E. G. Ross helped to prepare the town for incorporation. As treasurer of the committee, Ben's name was found on abstract papers as late as 1958. It was land on which the Assemblies of God Church Camp is now located. Many houses still standing in Mountainair and other New Mexico towns were built with Ben's lumber. (I joined the Mountainair Centennial Celebrations in 2003 in honor of my grandfather.)

In the teen years of Ben's youngest four boys, he did not push his sawmill operation with such gusto; he was older. At times, he would call his sons and say, "The beans are low, boys, let's go cut some boards." When the meat supply got low, he would say, "Boys, it is about time to make a trip to Miller's Ridge." For evening entertainment, Ben and his sons held "kangaroo court." A judge and lawyers were appointed, and they chose a cause or situation and argued the case, sometimes almost coming to blows. This heated competition continued throughout life.

It was ironic that on June 11, 1923, Benjamin Boyd Spencer was killed on the very railroad for which he had furnished crossties; he was sixty-nine. A Santa Fe passenger train struck his pickup west of Mountainair at Abo crossing and carried it a half-mile. He and his youngest son, Roy, were on their way to visit Ben's older daughter, Maude. My Uncle Roy was sixteen. Both men were severely injured. The passenger train took them to Albuquerque for medical aid. Uncle Roy said, "I knew the moment when my father died beside me." A pencil from Ben's own vest pocket pierced his heart. Uncle Roy lived the rest of his life with one leg much shorter than the other. Yet he married, fathered a family of seven children, and outlived all of Ben's other eight children. Roy was judge in Torrance County for sixteen years.

The Kaisers, Purcellas, and Hewetts were neighbors of the Spencers at East View. Uncle Roy married into the Hewett family. My dad, Charles, met Lilly Purcella in 1985 at the post office in Mountainair, where he had retired. She knew him, and this seemed to please him. He often spoke of Little Joe Purcella. One of the Kaiser family, or a hired worker, rode a fast horse, with the working harness still on it, to inform my Grandmother Sarah that Ben had died at St. Josephs Hospital. Sarah and her uninjured sons went to Albuquerque and buried Ben on South Yale Street. My older sister, Louella Mae, was seven months old when Grandpa Spencer was killed. He adored that redheaded granddaughter. He never saw me; I was born eleven months later. Grandpa already had grandchildren from his earlier family with Ida. I knew only one, Anne; she and her daughter, Lois, were nurses like me.

## My Grandmother, Sarah Ellen Adkins II Spencer

In Oklahoma, John Floyd Adkins, born September 13, 1835, married Sarah Ellen I, born January 17, 1842. She had been previously married to his cousin, Philip. Philip died, but not before the couple had produced one daughter named Florence Philip on July 12, 1862. That name was given to identify and memorialize her father. While I was a child, Dad's Aunt Flora Philip and her husband, Uncle Richard Guy Green, lived in Albuquerque. They had two daughters, Mabel (Green) Brown and Marie (Green) Leahrman, and a son, Melvin Guy. He was employed by the railroad and died at age forty-two in a train wreck. The other children of Sarah Ellen I and John Floyd Adkins were Anna Belle (Townsend), born January 7, 1868; Sarah Ellen II (my Grandmother Spencer), born May 8, 1869; John Albert, born March 22, 1872; Della Olive (Carpenter), born February 26, 1875; Laura Mae (Forney), born August 12, 1876; James Garfield, born October 3, 1878 and who lived two months; Parker Floyd, born August 15, 1879; Minnie Lula (Hoff), born December 1, 1880; Oscar, born March 10, 1883 and who lived four months; Alice Delpha, born June 6, 1885 and who lived six years. At some point in time, part of the John Floyd Adkins family moved to Kansas. What a strange feeling of deja vu I had as I stood in Hays, Kansas, in 1967. I had often heard Grandmother Sarah II tell about the Hays Teachers Normal where she received her training. Here I was in 1967, speaking in the College of Nursing at Hays State University about nursing in Africa. I was the guest of Professor Ruby Johnson in obstetrics. She had also nursed at clinics for the Konkomba and Bimoba Tribes of West Africa; we shared experiences.

The incident was similar to the one involving my grandfather and Medicine Lodge! I was a graduate of the University of New Mexico College of Nursing and was teaching in a school of nursing in Wichita. I was standing where Grandmother Sarah II once stood.

⌒

In 1896, young Sarah Ellen Adkins II, with ten years of teaching experience, left her family in Kansas and Oklahoma and headed for California alone. She was single and restless. The West sounded interesting to her—a little wild. In Albuquerque, New Mexico Territory, she got off the train for a quick look at the enchanted town. She met an interesting man named Ben Spencer. He had come to the Wells Fargo Office, next door to the Santa Fe train depot, to collect a shipment of coins to pay his sawmill employees. He was looking for a teacher for the Manzano area. Many of his sawmill workers had children; they needed a school. Ben persuaded Sarah to be the solution to that problem. They drove back along the rough dusty road in a buggy drawn rather swiftly by Chief and Blue. That sixty miles must have seemed an eternity to Sarah, and the Manzanos must have seemed very high and frightening, but beautiful, to this young flatland lady. She boarded with Ben's mother and taught school in one room of Ben's commissary wherever Ben's sawmill took them. The isolation of the mountains could have been unbearable, but work kept away boredom. She was in an unfamiliar land that had no electricity, a wood stove for cooking, and a stream or well for water. (Who better to understand this situation than I, her granddaughter? I made a similar journey north in the Gold Coast of West Africa in 1954 when I was young and single.)

After Ben Spencer's second wife died back East, he decided that he liked independent, young Sarah from Kansas. He persuaded her to become his wife. They were married in Albuquerque, May 2, 1898. Their first son, Floyd, was born at Escabosa, February 2, 1900, before they moved back south to the Manzano Mountains where Ben had previously had sawmills. Sarah assumed more responsibilities. The area needed a post office and an official name; Sarah named it East View. Sarah and Ben's other three sons, Charles, John, and Roy, were born in East View.

The view east over the Manzano foothills to the Estancia Valley was endless. Sarah tended the commissary. They sold prunes and coconut at the commissary, and in later years, I heard my father and Uncle Floyd tell how they gorged on the two items until they were ill. My dad never allowed my mom to put coconut in our desserts. Uncle Floyd would never eat prunes.) At times, Sarah's school was in their home, especially while she was having her own four boys. Sarah said Mollie Corbett taught one year when Ben's aged mother needed extra care, and that helped.

Sarah's background included a strong Christian faith. She fed her faith by reading the Bible. She tells of a definite place out among cedar trees where she prayed often and of the deep experiences she had with God, as He became her strength. While Ben did not wax eloquent about his Christian faith, he provided food and a place for the circuit-riding Preacher Means to preach. He preached in Ben's commissary on Sundays, and Sarah took her sons. Dances were held in Ben's commissary on Saturday nights, and Ben went. The grave of Preacher Means is near Ben's in Albuquerque on South Yale Street.

I've heard the four boys tell of how they helped Ben at the sawmill, but not much was said about what they did to help Sarah; she had no girls to help. However, in a letter from Charles going to high school in Colorado to his brother, Roy, he admonishes, "Dry the dishes and carry wood for mother." Sarah often told a story about her youngest. When Roy was near courting age, she told him, "Marry for love; never for money." He replied, "But if she has money, how I can love her!"

As a teacher, Sarah had many sayings, and she passed them on to her sons and students. Charles, my dad, passed some on to us. One was the familiar, "Oh, what a tangled web we weave when once we practice to deceive." Another was, "Never whittle toward yourself boys, and you'll never cut yourself." They were simple but pragmatic. On proving a point, she told how they had a circle grindstone to sharpen household or sawmill items. It was missing, and someone, in an attempt to avoid blame, said, "Well, I've told you before that if you left that grindstone out there, an old cow would eat it." Ben's older children and even their children, had Sarah as their teacher, since they lived nearby. Jim's daughter, Anne, told me, "In school, Sarah was very partial to her four sons." When the family made trips to Mountainair and back to East View in a slow rolling wagon or a swift buggy, Ben, Sarah, the boys, or the passengers would sing: "Molly, Oh, Molly I've told you before, make me a pallet, I'll sleep on the floor;" "Write me a letter, send it by mail; send it in care of the Birmingham jail;" "The daring young man on the flying trapeze;" or "The bird in a gilded cage." Time would pass swiftly. The closer to home they got, the thicker the foliage and higher the graceful pine trees became. The rocky Manzano Mountains were so near!

On June 11, 1923, the message of Ben's accident reached Sarah. The letters she wrote to her sisters and mother revealed her grief. She wrote, "The boys came with me to Albuquerque, where we buried Ben. It was a very sad time for us. The boys went back to Mountainair the next day. I will stay with Sister Flora (Philip) Green while young Roy is in the hospital with the severely crushed leg. The nurses say Ben's chest and hips were crushed, and his pencil pierced his heart; they say he suffered!"

Sarah, only fifty-four, never remarried. She watched her four sons marry and her grandchildren grow. Her first son, Robert Floyd, married Maxine Hawkins in 1936; they had no children. He worked in mines and sawmills. He died in 1948 at age forty-eight. His mother outlived him by five years. Charles married Edna Mae Layman in January 1921. They had four children: Louella, Charlese (me), Calvin, and Royce. He and Edna pastored churches and owned mom and pop businesses. Charles died in 1989; he was 88. Sarah's son John Franklin married Dee Swope in 1925. They had four girls: Mamie Jo, Johnye Fern, Frances, and Betty. John was a hard worker in construction. He died in 1976 at age seventy-two. Roy Adkins married Mabel Autry in 1926. They had seven children: Barbara, Helen, Verna, Roy Jr., Dixie Jo, Patricia, and Richard. Roy was a barber, storekeeper, and judge in Torrance County. He died at Christmastime in 1993 at age eighty-seven.

Sarah Spencer lived her last few years in Belen, New Mexico, in an apartment connected to the home of my parents, Charles and Edna. She ate her noon meal with them. She used a knife in one hand and a fork in the other to eat. She called her dress suit a costume. This was strange to me, until I went to school in England. I saw the Continental way of eating and heard people there talk about their costume for dress-up and church. I learned that Mother Spencer was very English and very proud of it. On one of my teenage visits with her, she wrote on lined notebook paper in pencil:

### Golden Keys

*A bunch of golden Keys is mine,*
*To make each day with gladness shine.*
*Good morning, that's the golden key,*
*That unlocks every day for me.*
*When evening comes, good night, I say,*
*And close the door of each glad day.*
*When at the table, If you please,*
*I take from off my bunch of keys.*

*Excuse me, beg your pardon, too,*
*When by mistake some harm I do.*
*Or if unkind harm I've given,*
*With forgive me, I shall be forgiven.*
*On a golden ring these keys I bind.*
*This is its motto: Be ye kind.*

—Unknown

Mother Spencer once told me, "I felt called to some special work for God. I told God I was not capable of doing what I had seen special people do for Him." She said He answered, "You could go to Chicago if I asked you to go." Chicago must have seemed like the end of the earth. Mother Spencer died on March 13, 1953. She would have been eighty-four in two months. At the funeral, the choir sang old hymns for over an hour. I think God has a sense of humor and the singing was for Sarah; she loved to sing! My grandmother, Sarah Ellen Adkins II Spencer, was buried in Mountainair beside her first son, Robert Floyd. Ben's name may be on the founding documents of the town, but Sarah worked beside him.

## My Father, Charles Spencer

Charles Spencer—that was my dad; he had no middle name. He, like me, was second child of four. He was born June 4, 1901, to Ben and Sarah Spencer in East View, New Mexico Territory. East View has always been a community of scattered ranch homes and sawmills, about sixteen miles west of Mountainair, in canyons and foothills, covered by pine, piñon, cedar and juniper trees. Dad said that on January 6, 1912, when New Mexico became the forty-seventh state in the Union, it was so cold that the greater celebration took place the following July Fourth. Charles was eleven years old.

Later in life, Charles sustained a fractured skull when struck by the butt of a gun. Afterwards, this often required removal of bone fragments from his head by the elder Dr. W. R. Lovelace in Albuquerque. Dr. Lovelace's medical practice had been in Willard until Mountainair, a few miles west, outgrew Willard. Dr. Lovelace moved his practice to Albuquerque. Dr. Randy Lovelace and Dr. Ed Lassetter were his nephews. Each time my dad was hospitalized, the elder Dr. Lovelace proudly told available doctors and nurses what a miracle Charles was. I own a book called *Men Of Space*, Volume 2 (Thomas 1939), which contains profiles of the leaders in space research, development and exploration. It has a foreward by Wernher von Braun. In it, Randy Lovelace wrote: "To Ed, a wonderful cousin, from Randy." In the 1960s, Dr. Lassetter wrote in it: "To Leonora Wister from her first job. Ed Lassetter." Aunt Leonora took care of Ed when he was a baby. On April 29, 1998, my aunt wrote on the same page: "I gratefully and lovingly pass this treasured book to my beloved niece, Charlese Spencer, RN, MN, SCM. She was with me when Ed gave the book to me and has nursed patients of Randy, Ed, and their beloved Uncle W. R. Lovelace. Alicia, Ed's mother, was a sister of the elder Dr. Lovelace. I knew Randy when he lived with his grandmother next door to the Lassetters. Signed: Leonora (Layman) Wister, Phoenix, AZ." Following page 106 in that book is a picture. Below it is written, "Two eminent doctors, W. Randolph Lovelace II and his friend, Charles Mayo. Some of Lovelace's important research was accomplished while he was in uniform in World War II." I prize the book highly.

Sarah Spencer, being a teacher, was concerned because a high school education was not available for their teenage sons. She sent them to live with two of her sisters, Minnie and Della. Floyd, her first, was sent to Oklahoma to live with Harry and Minnie Hoff and cousins Alma and Lloyd while going to high school. Charles went to live with Frank and Della Carpenter and their son, Frank Jr. for high school in

Montrose, Colorado. The Carpenters once had a sheep ranch in the Estancia valley before moving to Colorado, so Charles knew them. However, Charles was not happy living away from home. His classes in Colorado included Spanish grammar, which did not sound like the Spanish he learned as a child. He lost a front tooth playing football, but he said it helped him to whistle tunes the rest of his life. I never saw my dad without that space until he got dentures. In January 1921, at the age of nineteen, Charles married Edna Mae Layman in Mountainair. They both continued to work with his parents at East View and lived in a room at the commissary. Almost two years later, to be near a doctor for the birth of Louella Mae, Charles and Edna moved into Ben's three-cornered town house in Mountainair. Edna's mother, Lula, was renting the Spencer Office Building as a residence just next door. By then, the Spencers did not need an office in town; the demand for lumber had waned. Four of Lula's six children still lived with her. On June 11, 1923, a seventh-year birthday party was taking place at the three-cornered house for Edna's young sister, Olivia Irene. My sister, Louella Mae, was almost eight months old. A panic-stricken messenger arrived to inform them that Ben and my dad's youngest brother, Roy, had been involved in the train-pickup collision. That ended the birthday party! This tragedy left Charles and Edna in great difficulty with their growing family. By May 1924, they had two daughters, Louella Mae and me. The Great Financial Depression was deep! By 1932, they had added two sons—Calvin Lee and Royce Ray. Mom and Dad sold fruit, hoed weeds in the bean fields, and became farmers. It is hard to imagine the drastic changes that faced my father. He was thrust from the tranquility of living in Eastview to being forced to move anywhere and often to find food and housing for a growing family. Life in the Wild West was primitive enough without a depression. My father, Charles, often quoted this poem he learned from his mother as part of his philosophy.

## The Three Were Envious

*A man in his carriage was riding along,*
*With his gaily dressed wife by his side.*
*In satin and lace she looked like a queen*
*And he like a king in his pride.*

*A woodcutter stood on the walk as they passed*
*And the carriage he carefully eyed.*
*And he said as he worked with his saw on the log,*
*I wish I were rich and could ride.*

*And the man in the carriage remarked to his wife,*
*There's one thing I'd do if I could,*
*I'd give all my wealth for the strength and the health*
*Of the man who is sawing the wood.*

It became my responsibility to care for Dad the last five years of his life. He went to church with me every Sunday that he was physically able. After a year in a senior mobile park in Albuquerque, Charles bought a house in Mountainair; he wanted to have a garden. Dad had traveled from the Pacific Ocean to the Atlantic and from Canada to Mexico. He had lived, worked, or owned property in most states in the western half of the United States. He chose to retire in Torrance County, New Mexico, where he, his brothers, and even his children were born. On Dad's birthday in 1988, we drove out to Eastview. There were houses still standing that were familiar to him. He talked as we rode along. "There is the old Hewett place," he said. He paused and then said, "The rock schoolhouse where both your mom and I went to school is just a mile north of here." We drove another mile west before the heavy barbed wire fence lining the road allowed us to turn north toward the house of Dad's birth. We stopped for a few minutes at the corner. Dad continued, "Now the Kaisers live right straight ahead. There is a deep canyon up there. My grandmother, Elizabeth Spencer, is buried right near here."

I looked high up into a stately pine tree, and there was a platform. I asked, "Dad, did you have a tree house?" He replied, "At one time or another." We turned the corner to go north. He said, "The land on the left toward the mountains belonged to Dad's older children. My half-brother, Jim, lived there with his family. His children attended the rock school with us." As we drove by the school and took pictures, Dad sighed and said softly, "I liked my niece, Annie; she was a nice girl. You know, we found her in Phoenix in the 1950s." When we arrived at the old Spencer house, we drove into the yard and parked out near an old barn that looked as if it were built with longer railroad crossties. Dad said, "That is the same ole barn, but a lot around here has changed." With nostalgia in his voice he added, "Many days, before we were married, your Mom and I walked one mile directly east from here to the rock school house." Then a smirk of humor flashed from Dad's eyes as he said, "I do not see the old outhouse. We four boys visited it every night at bedtime with our father; we had no indoor plumbing." It suddenly struck me as a humorous dichotomy that there were solar panels on the roof and a butane tank behind the house. I half expected to see the old grindstone out behind the house, but perhaps a cow did eat it! There was a hole in the ground, which could have collected water for a boiler. Dad said, "Oh, we had sawmills in several places. My dad, Ben, had a saw-mill in Barranca Canyon even before any of us four boys were born. Dad moved his sawmill from there to Escabosa." He said, "We had a sawmill in Guiterra Canyon. There we had a camping outfit only. At the bottom of Ox Canyon we had a sawmill and a rough old house. North of here at the sienega, we had the little mill." Dad seldom talked so much; he was remembering, "I think our commissary was located at the sienega. Your mom and I lived there in one room when Mae was small. That was before you were born. One day, I threw

my pocketknife and split a cat's head when it got on our dining table. I told your mom not to look as she was pregnant
with you." I was born with a brown birthmark on my thigh
that I always called a Scottie dog. I never convinced Mom;
she said it was the cat! Dad and I tried to drive north and
west to the sienega, but it was fenced as if privately owned,
so we drove back to Mountainair. Dad continued to talk,
"See those miles of fence posts? I'm sure my dad put those
in the ground over eighty years ago." We were brought back
to reality when a rock slipped off a tire and hit up under my
car, sounding like a gunshot. I watched the oil gauge back to
Dad's home in Mountainair and another hour to Albuquerque. A hole was indeed found in the oil pan, but up high, so
the engine was not damaged. Oh, the woes of civilization! At
least we didn't have to feed the horses when we got home!

On June 4, 1989, for Dad's eighty-eighth birthday, I took
him on a nostalgic journey to where we had lived in Tererro,
New Mexico, on the Pecos River in the 1930s. We crossed
the Pecos River on a new metal bridge; the old one next
to it that we once used was now a pedestrian bridge. We
stopped at the entrance of Indian Creek, but it was fenced,
so we could not get up the canyon to where we had lived
at the sawmill when I was eleven. Dad even snapped some
of the pictures we took at the Brush Ranch. We drove back
across the mountain to Las Vegas to visit friends, Eddie and
Kathy (Martinez) King. That evening, we attended the kin-
dergarden graduation of their daughter, Krystle. She called
my dad, "Grandpa," and was very careful and attentive to
him because he was tottery as he walked.

It was almost midnight when we got back to Dad's house
in Mountainair. He said, "Don't you think you are too tired
to drive on to Albuquerque tonight?" I had been gone over
a week, so I drove on home. I slept late the next morning,
as I was tired. In Mountainair, my dad went to bed as soon
as I left him. The next day, on June 5, he was in his garden
using a matic hoe to dig up asparagus or rhubarb that had

spread out of bounds. He had a heart attack. It was one day after his eighty-eighth birthday. His neighbor, Fidel Lovato, brought him over the Manzano Mountains to Lovelace Medical Center in Albuquerque and phoned me about 8:00 P.M. For the following week, I practically lived at Lovelace Hospital. The doctor told Dad that a pattern for the elderly was that they might have a second heart attack before the heart muscle was healed enough to cope wth it. He asked Dad if he wanted to be put on life support if he could not breathe on his own. Dad answered, "No, when my Lord calls, I am ready; I do not want to be kept here by man." My brother, Calvin, and his wife, Yvonne, had already made airline reservations for their annual vacation to come from Seattle to visit Dad and Mom; no changes were needed. God planned ahead for Dad! That was a far cry from the wagon train journey Grandfather Ben made from Illinois that started all this. Dad did indeed have a second heart attack six days after the first one. He did not survive. Charles had lived a full life, in his way and in the free American West. He died, aged eighty-eight, on June 11, the same date as his father's death sixty-five years before. There was even a birthday party for Mom's younger sister, Irene. At Grandpa Ben's death, I was not even born. This time, I stayed with Dad while the others went to the birthday party in Hillsboro, New Mexico. The following was written for the family reunion in 1984 and read again at Dad's funeral in 1989.

## An Ode to Charles Spencer

*Charles was born second son of four,*
*To Sarah just four, but to Ben several more.*
*The Manzanos were home—a sawmill his cradle.*
*Ben ruled the kingdom; Sarah taught them the Bible.*
*The boys lost their father, as tragedies struck.*
*With security gone, they seemed down on their luck.*
*Charles took a bride, little more than a child.*
*He grew a thick hide as the West was still wild.*
*With four babes of his own—Great Depression rampant,*
*By sawmill or in business, there was food, seldom scant.*
*To Christ he bowed his will in 1937.*
*From then unto the end his thoughts were miracles and heaven.*
*Tingley Hospital meant employment—and Pearl Harbor too.*
*Lean years left behind, dimmed the sorrows he knew.*
*WW II brought prosperity and churches—he pastored a few.*
*His grandkids meant enjoyment and the years fairly flew.*
*Today as we give to our father this ode,*
*The lives we now live still echo his mode.*

—Lovingly, Daughter Elsie Charlese Spencer 6/84, 6/89

JANUARY 1993    ROCKS, WOOD, SOIL AND TOIL -- White Oaks Homestead
*Pen and ink by southwestern artist, Carl E. Ness of Alamogordo, N.M.*
This rock structure with a dirt roof was constructed in the late 1800s in White Oaks, N.M. The door and window frames were made from local lumber as well. For more information on this and other prints call (505)437-1134.

1. Celebrating statehood, 1912, July 4. Ben Spencer standing. Roy with hand on Sarah's knee. 2. Note solar panels on old home, cookout stove, cable roll for table and log barn. 3. Celebration at Ben's sawmill, 1912 statehood. Ben and son, John, at end of walk; son, Floyd, on platform left of walk; Sarah and son, Charles, (five right of walk). 4. Note old site of sawmill and residual dam for water power, with TV dish and butane tank. 5. Ben with daughter, Maude. 6. Dow Store at Chilili.

1.Ben's and Sarah's four sons. Back right: Floyd and Charles. Front: John F. and Roy A. 2. Sarah's teaching permit in New Mexico. 3. Floyd in school with cousin Lloyd Hoff in Kansas. 4. Floyd's own New Mexico horse brand. 5. Charles in school in Colorado. 6. Charles back in New Mexico, married Edna M. Layman, 1921. 7. Letter Sarah wrote the day Ben died.

# CHAPTER 2

## My Layman-Cox Roots

### My Grandfather, Charles Layman

CHARLES EDWARD LAYMAN WAS born May 20, 1884, at Dublin, Texas, in Erath County a few miles southwest of Dallas. I graduated from high school in Fort Worth and from college in Waxahachie, Texas. Neither town is far from his birthplace. For different reasons I never saw either of my grandfathers; their lives affected my parents, Charles Spencer and Edna Layman, and thus affected me.

D. G. Layman, born Oct. 27, 1845, and his wife, Mary Sue Eddy, born June 10, 1854, came from West Virginia, via Missouri and Oklahoma, to the Dallas, Texas, area. They had nine children: Daisy, born April 10, 1875; Minor Gilmer, born December 25, 1878; Samantha Lorene, born August 16, 1880; Charles Edward, my grandfather, born May 20, 1884; Mary Margaret (Molly), born August 16, 1885; Bertha M., born March 14, 1888, but died young; Hattie Virginia, born August 25, 1889; Silas Sam, born September 10, 1891; Walter Lee, born April 5, 1894. Walter and others of this family moved to South Texas. One had a daughter who married Lawyer Ebheart in San Antonio. While building them a home, he stepped on a nail and died of tetanus. His in-law parents, D. G. and Mary Layman, went west and bought a ranch at Tahoka, Texas. Their son, Charles, started his own herd of cattle one hundred miles north of Tahoka near Paladura Canyon.

Charles Edward Layman and Luella Mae Cox, my grandparents, were married in 1904 at the First Baptist Church in Amarillo, Texas. My mother, Edna, was their first child, born in Canyon City, Texas, July 25, 1905. The word *City* has been dropped from the maps. Edna was little more than a newborn when Charles and Lula went on a cattle drive and wagon train from Canyon to an area sixty miles west of Tahoka. The cattle drive may have included the W. J. Luna family, also from Paladura Canyon. They are considered "founders of the town of Plains in 1907." In July of 1995, I met two granddaughters of W. J. Luna, Wilma (Luna) Powell and Mary Jo (Luna) St. Romain, still living in Plains. They were busy with a museum, ranching, and committees.

Charles and Lula Layman lived in and around Plains, Texas, while they were having the rest of their family. They lived at ranches where Charles worked, or on land they owned. From 1906 to 1915, the records show that Charles and Lula bought land from, sold land to, or traded land with people named Bess, Cruckshank, Luna, Beeson, Roberts, Brown, Shaw, and King. A Mr. Williams recorded some of this in Roswell, New Mexico. Charles was a rancher and freighted from Big Spring, Texas, on the east, across the New Mexico border, and west beyond Roswell. He would drive away with a horsedrawn wagon loaded with farm produce or animals and come back days later with other animals, a piano, or shoes for the children. He hauled lumber from Big Spring for private homes, Tingley General Store in Plains, and the first Plains Court House. That courthouse burned; the one now in use is the third. My last "roots" visit to Plains was October 2002 with my brother, Calvin Lee. The land around Plains appears unproductive; with water, much of the area could flourish with agriculture. It could feed cattle.

Not many owners have been challenged to see what else it could do; since the mid-1930s they have "laughed all the way to the bank" with oil money.

My Grandfather Charles was often gone from the home. Lula was not happy to be alone so much. When Charles returned, he wanted to rest. She had been tied to the home with children and chores; she longed for social events. They had disagreements about many things. However, he and Lula had a total of six children between 1905 and 1916. Edna Mae, my mother, was born in Canyon City July 25, 1905. Leonora, the first baby born in the Town of Plains, Texas, was born July 24, 1907. Talbert Jackson was born when their dad was a working cowboy at the Tarver Ranch in 1909. John Coyle was born on a visit back to Canyon City in 1910. Charlcie Elaine was born on the D. G. Layman ranch near Tahoka in 1911. Olivia Irene was born June 11, 1916, in Warren, New Mexico. Records reflect that in 1912, Charles traded land he owned in the Plains, Texas, area for land southwest of Bronco, just inside New Mexico. At first, they had a one-room rock house over a cellar. My mother, Edna, and her sister, Leonora, started their formal schooling. They walked a mile southeast to Murphy's Chapel School. On one of Charles' trips he brought home a pinkish burro named Jenny and her baby. Edna then rode the mother and Leonora rode the baby. When Jack started to school, the two girls doubled up on Jenny and Jack rode the baby.

Gilmer Layman, who freighted with his brother, Charles, lived about a half mile southeast of Murphy's Chapel with his wife, Clara Bell, and family. For some time, Edna and her siblings had cousins Terril, Clarence, Ernest, Dalton, and baby Blanch to play with. Then, Gilmer moved his family to Hobbs, New Mexico, where Meta Clara, their next child, was born in 1913. The rest of Gilmer's family, Eddie Lee, twins Earl and Arel, Sue, James, and Beulah, were born in Castro County, Texas. The family moved to Hereford in Deaf Smith County and had a business for years.

My Grandfather Charles continued to freight alone. He used two wagons hitched together and eight mules to pull them. He hauled lumber for new building construction and cottonseed meal and cake for stock feed. In 1914 he bought an eighteen-foot-square room at Elida, New Mexico, and moved it over sixty miles on skids and freight wagons to the Bronco house to make an upstairs bedroom for Lula and him. Bedrooms for the children were downstairs. Charles and Lula had neighbors on all sides, but none nearby. Harv Harris and wife had a store and post office on the State Line at Bronco. Other ranchers were the H. Fields, the Baldy Smiths, the Cochs (Cooks), and the Wardens. The Claude Odles' daughter, Elva, was Lula's age. The Randolph Rampys lived farther south. Special friends were the Arthur Davis family and Walter and Ellen Patterson. It was a two-way friendship, as Walter was known to borrow a stud bull from Charles. Ellen was a teacher like Lula. Sam Dixon drilled two wells side-by-side for Charles. Charles constructed a walking beam for the tandem wells, so when the beam went down on one end, it pulled water up from the other well.

Grandpa Charles was a rancher's working cowboy, not a gun-toting cowboy. Lula was the epitome of a hardy frontier mother. She planted fruit trees, shade trees, flowers, and vegetables. Their cellar was full of canned food. Lula raised ducks, chickens, turkeys, and guinea foul. Edna and Leonora said their happiest, but shortest, time in childhood was while they attended school at Murphy's Chapel, but Charles suddenly sold the unfinished place to J. King. With all this, why would Charles sell and move? He used physical force to get Lula's signature to sell the Bronco house. In Texas, he could sell anything they had with his signature. In New Mexico, he needed her signature, so that was the only item Lula had to sign. She was so upset over the sale of her home that she said she lost heart. They moved into a spacious house in Warren, New Mexico. The Warren Store and Post Office had moved, as the road through town was relocated. Warren was removed from maps. This doubled the distance the children had to walk to Murphy's Chapel School in winter. Rumors included betrayal and hot tempers of both sides.

On April 28, 1916, Lula's birthday, Charles came home driving a two-seated Ford car with the top down. In the book, *Yoakum County History 1907-1954*, I found that a J. King had bought a Ford in December 1914, and then in 1916, he bought a Buick. The Ford may have been used as partial payment on the Bronco house he bought from Grandpa Charles that same year. When Charles arrived in Warren late that evening, he found Lula and some of the children putting horses in the corral. He asked, "Why?" Lula said, "To have the horses available so we can go to town tomorrow to buy cloth to sew baby clothes." Charles turned the horses out; a conflict erupted, and he packed his suitcase as Lula unpacked it. Finally, he left. He returned momentarily and went to the barn to get a tarpaulin. Lula sent an older child out to his car to get his suitcase; Charles left without his clothing.

This was just two months before the birth of their sixth and last baby, Olivia, on June 11. Charles was thirty-two. Lula discovered that he had mortgaged some cows and thirty-three of their thirty-seven horses. He had been gradually selling what land they owned in Texas without Lula's signature. He took all but a $250 note that was due in 1917 and left. He may have had more than $2,000 with him; that was a lot of money in 1916. Mr. Townsend, to whom he had mortgaged the animals, came and collected them. Some of the children received postcards from their father on their next birthday. The picture on the postcards was Charles standing on a California pier. Lula received a postcard that is still controversial. It seems that he asked Lula if she would bring the children and go to Peru with him. She replied that it would be impossible for her to take six children to South America. The correspondence stopped. Most of his children (my mother and part of my five aunts and uncles) believed that he just forgot to dot his "i" so that it looked as if he were asking them to go to Peru when he was actually asking them to go to Lake Piru, just north of Los Angeles. This made more sense because he had actually purchased land at Lake Piru.

The First World War followed, and then there was a great influenza epidemic in 1918. My mom often said she believed her father died in that. She was angry because he left her mother with six children to feed. She felt that by his leaving, he threw her away; that made her a nothing. All six children showed anger in their way. Leonora Layman-Wister believed she was special to her father, so she asked, "Why would he leave me?" She and Jack lived in Los Angeles during their teen years. They were there to make a living, but also to look for their father, who was less than fifty miles north of them.

Jack was a middle child, too young to work for a living and too old to stay at home with the younger ones. He was caught stealing money at an early age; he gave some to his mom. In some cases, he was not guilty, but falsely accused, and served prison time. Wherever he was, I wrote letters; he answered some. Uncle Johnny told me, "I had to work to help feed the family, even while I was going to school. To have shoes, I held out money from my paper route. Each evening, I hid the shoes on a crossbeam under a bridge and went back next morning to put them on for school." At times, he seemed angry with the whole family, yet at his wife's funeral, he cried and said to me, "I loved my family."

Charlcie Elaine Layman-Hallsworth married early. Anger and loneliness turned her to alcohol, and she died in California at 49, the first of the six children to die. Olivia Irene Layman-Franklin was born after her father left. To her, he was saying, "You are none of mine," so her non-verbal reply was, "I am none of yours."

Charles must have been terribly hurt and angry that Lula refused to bring the children and go with him anywhere. He might have thought that in California he could start over and make a living for the large family. When he knew it was not to be, he chose another route for his life. In the fall of 1983, after fifty-seven years, the death certificate of Charles Edward Layman arrived in my Albuquerque mailbox addressed to Edna, my mom. It was from her sister, Leonora, in Phoenix. Her oldest grandson, James Lester, married a girl, Carolyn, who was into genealogy. She discovered a death certificate for my grandfather in Ventura County, north of Los Angeles, California. The place of death was stated "Piru." My grandfather had gone to Piru, not Peru! Perhaps the fate of an entire family of six children rested on an un-dotted *i* on a postcard. The true scenario of this tragedy went to the grave with my grandfather. An interesting item on that death certificate was the date of death, April 11, 1928; he was only 44 years old. The cause of death read, "Injury to head and chest when struck by a Santa Fe train at Piru Crossing, in Ventura County." Yes, this was almost the same wording as on the death certificate of my Grandpa Spencer at Abo crossing in New Mexico just five years before.

In April 1984, soon after we received the certificate of my Grandpa Layman's death, Aunt Leonora asked Mom and me to take a trip in her Honey motor home. I was on crutches and wore a neck brace because of the newly diagnosed arachanoiditis, an incurable neuro-muscular disorder. Travel would be difficult, but we decided to go. Our first stop was Piru, California. We looked in a phone book and found the name Don Layman. We phoned them. Reluctantly, they agreed to talk with us. Leonora, at age seventy-six, maneuvered the huge Honey up the steep, partially paved, winding road. As we topped the hill, we saw a beautiful lake. We had to check in at a tollhouse and were allowed to enter free as guests of the Laymans, who lived at lakeside. We went up another precarious escarpment, where we parked in their yard. Mom refused to go in. "They had my dad; I did not!" she lashed out. Leonora and I went to the house and knocked. Inside we met Don and Jean. We stated our

mission and again met anger. Don said flatly, "My father
had no other family before he married our mom!" Pictures
were compared, and it became evident that we were speaking of the same person, Charles Edward Layman. We cried
a bit. Don and Jean were indeed the children of Charles, my
grandfather. We discovered that they were also angry; their
father had left their mother to raise them from an early age.
When Charles was killed in 1928 Don was only five; Jean
was three. My new Uncle Don was one year older than I;
Aunt Jean was one year younger than I. They both had children. I went out to the Honey and explained to Edna, "Mom,
they are as angry as you are." She went in, and we talked for
hours.

We slept that night in the Honey. In the morning, we
took pictures with them and their children. Don had to go
check on the grazing cattle; Jean had to go to work at the
tollhouse. They directed us to my grandfather's grave at
Bardsdale Cemetery near Fillmore, in Ventura County, California. We went there, visited, and took pictures. The grave-
stone simply said, "Charles E. Layman, 1886-1928." He was
really born in 1884. It was somewhat of a closure for Edna,
Leonora, and me; we knew where he was. We continued our
tour to northern California, Oregon, and Washington State
to visit children of Edna and Leonora.

Our newfound relatives from Piru have come to visit us.
On one trip in 1991, my Aunt Leonora took them to Earth,
Texas, to visit with our Uncle Sam Layman. He was a brother to their dad, Charles. Uncle Sam was celebrating his one
hundredth birthday. He got a letter of congratulation from
President Ronald Reagan. Sam still had his own teeth. The
fluoride in that west Texas water may discolor your teeth,
but it must be terribly healthy. West Texans not only die with
their boots on, they die with their own teeth in their mouth.
Uncle Sam became special to our family since we had no
Charles Layman. He and Aunt Bessie had four children: Ar-
lyne, Donald, Clifford, and L. G. Uncle Sam and Aunt Bes-

sie had close friends named Elzie and Ophelia (Willingham) Williams. I learned that they were the grandparents of Spain Trask, who helped keep my computer running during the writing of this book. The Williamses and Laymans are buried in the Lasbuddy Cemetery near Earth, and Muleshoe, Texas. Spain and Bettye Trask are missionaries to Fiji in the 2000s.

## My Grandmother, Lula Mae Cox-Layman

I never saw either of my grandfathers. My two grandmothers played an extremely visible role in my childhood. Grandmother Luella Mae Cox was born in Abilene, Texas, on April 28, 1885. Her parents moved to Canyon City, Texas, soon after her birth. As a young adult, Lula helped to create and market ladies hats. Along with the family, she taught elocution, a form of speech therapy. She assisted her private students to improve diction, expression, and delivery of speech. Her father, John Jones Cox, (born Griffin—a French name), actually came from Canada for diction lessons and stayed to marry Lula's mother, Sarah Jane Roberts (Cherokee and Irish). John J. Cox served honorably as a Texas Ranger and in the Confederate Army. They had ten children. The first three were Nancy, Bill, Ellie Heald, (who had John, Jack, and Laura Heald-Zimlich.) Ellie died when her three were young. The Cox's fourth was Lorena Cox-Maahs, (who had little Lorena, Evelyna, and Edwina Maahs-Cage.) When Ellie died, Lorena Maahs raised her niece, Laura Heald, along with her own daughters. The fifth Cox child was Myrtle Potter, often called Molly. The sixth was my grandmother, Luella Mae Cox-Layman, usually called Lula. Dock was seventh; he married and was a musician. Sam Cox, eighth child, never married, lived at home, and died of skin cancer. At some point, a set of twins, who died soon after birth, made the ten.

Lula Mae Cox and Charles Edward Layman, my grandparents, were married in Amarillo. Their first child, Edna (my mother), was born in the Cox home in Canyon City. Leonora was born after the cattle drive to Plains, Texas, and was called Edna's "second-year birthday present." Jack, Johnny, Charlcie, and Olivia were born in the next nine years. Charles and Lula, this young, vigorous, bombastic couple, faced adversity consistently during those twelve years of marriage. Edna was born with a clubfoot, and Leonora did not breathe quickly at birth. They lived in a tent when Jack was born. The family traveled over a hundred miles, by covered wagon, back to Canyon City for Johnny's birth.

Back in Plains, when Johnny was still an infant, Jack became very ill with what my mother called *colum infantum.* It could have been cholera, typhoid, or diphtheria; he was less than two years old. Jack's illness became apparent one day when he pulled on Lula's apron, cried, and begged to be picked up. Lula's hands were covered with biscuit dough, so she said, "Just a minute," but Jack fainted. Lula grabbed him by the feet and shook him until he cried. Almost immediately following Jack's illness, Charles and Lula had typhoid fever. Since Lula was ill, Johnny, just three months old, was weaned and fed by spoon; there were no bottles. Charles's parents came from Tahoka, east of Plains, to help during the illness. When the relatives were convinced that Charles and Lula could not hear and that they were going to die, they discussed division of the children. Lula heard them and prayed that God would let her live to raise their children; He did. When Charlcie, their fifth child, was a newborn, Johnny became critically ill. Lula sent for a medication called Calomel. She said they sent belladonna by mistake, and Johnny convulsed and almost died. His growth was thwarted for life. When Johnny was almost four years old, he lifted an axe to cut a harness that was too big for his colt. Charlcie did not want it cut and reached for it; the axe hit her head. Her head was split, and Lula thought she could see the child's brain. Edna was sent to the Odles to phone the doctor. Receivers were lifted on party lines; they thought Edna said Charles had been injured. People came from every direction with food. Charles was freighting and not at home. Mrs. Rogers held Charlcie while Doctor Rump stitched the wound. Blanche Harris held Johnny; he was so distraught about what he had done. People stayed to eat, and they made it a social event. The children pulled taffy.

Considering the above scenario, it would have taken a miracle to hold their marriage together. The Warren house had a big front room, one big room for kitchen and dining downstairs, and two bedrooms upstairs. Lula was still stressed from leaving the Bronco house and pregnant again when Charles left. Two months later, a woman they called Aunt Georgia Bess helped to delivered Olivia, the last baby, and stayed with Lula for a while to help with housework and care of the children. As pay, Lula gave her the shirt and suit Charles had left behind in his suitcase.

Lula could not afford to stay in this better house with six children, so they moved again. Lula traded cattle for one-half section of land from a Harley Foster on top of the Cap Rock, in the Llano Estacado (Stockaded Plains) east of Roswell, New Mexico. It had a windmill and a three-room mud and rock house with rough board floors. The five older children walked four miles south daily to the Mescalero School. In the spring of 1917, the government required their cattle to be dipped. A fierce late storm struck and the wet, cold cows piled up in a corner of the fenced pasture and froze. State officials informed Lula that she had bought state selected land and that the seller knew it. The state also knew about the oil under the Cap Rock. Lula was given about three hundred dollars for the land and told to leave. She moved into Roswell, New Mexico, with her children and got a job at the Guilder Hotel for ten dollars per week. With six children in a ten-dollar-a-month rooming house on Virginia Avenue in Roswell, Lula would cook a pan of cornbread without eggs and put it on a shelf above the stove. When the children got hungry while she was at work, they could break off a piece. There was no social welfare to help. Edna, being oldest, cared for Olivia, the youngest. The children were so near the same age that fierce battles occurred between them. Mrs. Rosie Clampet and her husband, who lived in the same building, lost their land on the Cap Rock too. They watched Lula's older children.

Lula met Mr. Willie Sheets, a well digger. He was conscripted by the government to work for the duration of WWI in the shipyards of Astoria, Oregon. Lula soon followed, taking Jack, Johnny, Charlcie, and Olivia to Oregon. Edna, age twelve, was left to do housework for Mrs. Fucin, who lived just under the Cap Rock east of Roswell. They had indoor plumbing; Edna was impressed. At first, Leonora, age eleven, was placed in the town of Caprock with Mr. and Mrs. Crossland to help with housework and in their store and post office. Leonora left, and Edna moved to Caprock to help the Crossland family. Both my mother and my aunt have related to me the depth of loneliness while missing father, mother, sisters, and brothers at such a young age. When WWI ended in 1919, Lula and Mr. Sheets settled in Socorro, New Mexico, on the Rio Grande River. Lula sent a letter asking Edna and Leonora to come. They traveled from Roswell on a night train, where they met a Mrs. Glick and here two daughters. The lady taught Edna to crochet; many people have enjoyed Edna's afghans. At Belen, the girls transferred to a train going south to Socorro. I asked Mom and Aunt Leonora about the reunion in Socorro. They could not remember; it was too traumatic.

Lula had a job in Socorro renting rooms for fifty cents a night at the Sickler Hotel. Her children also had jobs. Jack and Johnny shined shoes. Edna went to Hilton's Hotel in San Marcial to sell beads. The children went to school. Hazel Loring was Edna's best friend. Her brother took Edna to her first movie. It was Mary Pickford and Douglas Fairbanks getting married by a preacher atop a church that collided with a house in rushing floodwater. She related the movie to her mother. The next morning, Lula was startled awake when she threw her hand over the edge of her bed into water. The family again lost everything they had, this time in the devastating 1919 Socorro Rio Grande flood. The Red Cross sent them east to Mountainair, a booming bean town just over the Manzano Mountains. Lula got a job cooking at a cafe. Leonora made beds in the two-story Abo Hotel near the Mountainair Train Depot. Edna went sixteen miles west of Mountainair to help Sarah Spencer with housework at East View. That was where she met Charles Spencer, Sarah and Ben's second son, who became her husband and my father.

Lula again became independent enough to support herself and those of her small children still at home. For years, she cooked and operated rooming or boarding houses in Albuquerque, Santa Fe, Laguna Pueblo, and Glorietta. When Lula's children lived in California during WWII, she moved there and was employed. Her children, despite their traumatic youth, actually did quite well. Edna Mae married my dad, and they had four children: Louella, Charlese, Calvin, and Royce. They owned mom-and-pop businesses and pastored a few churches. Aunt Leonora married Nevin Wister and had three children: Lester Layman, Robert Bruce, and Katherine Irene. Lester served with honors as a pilot in WWII and became a lawyer. Robert is a brainy inventor and consultant, and Katherine is a banker. These three are my only blood cousins from the six Layman children. Uncle Jack, after all his anger, married but had no children. He and his wife owned apartment houses in El Paso and traveled worldwide. He died before we found his father; he never knew! Uncle Johnny married Lois Garret. They had no children. They owned auto part stores in California. Lois was the niece of Sheriff Garret who shot Billy the Kid. Aunt Charlcie married B. Hallsworth and lived most of her adult life in California. She had no living children. Aunt Olivia worked in a bank in San Francisco during WWII. She owned a beauty shop in New Mexico, where she found a family when she married B Franklin in Hillsboro, adding my cousins Sonya, Saundra, Dennis, Troy, and Sharon.

After WWII, my Mamaw Lula Layman retired in Hot Springs, New Mexico. While she lived there, Ralph Edwards convinced the town to change its name to Truth or Consequences, the name of a TV show. I loved to visit my Mamaw Layman in TorC. She was witty; we laughed a lot. We went walking with her dogs over the sandy hills, and it reminded me of walking my dog, Ebony, down the Nakpanduri Escarpment in Africa. Once, as we walked, Lula said, "Charlese, I know what you mean when you call things 'worldly,' as there are certain things that separate us from the presence and approval of God." This must have been something she felt was special from God, as she was not one to share her inner feelings. Then, I learned that she had gone to church and had been baptized. Lula, my Mamaw Layman, died in TorC on Memorial Day, 1976, at the age of ninety-one while I was in Ghana, West Africa. Jack and Charlcie, two of Lula's children, preceded her in death. She said, "If my children are going to die, then I am ready to go also." Johnny and Edna died after Lula did. Two of her children are alive even as I write in 2003, my Aunt Leonora, next to the oldest (who still has her own teeth), and Olivia Irene, the youngest, who lives in Hillsboro, New Mexico. Both live alone.

## My Mother, Edna Mae Layman-Spencer

Edna Mae Layman-Spencer, that was my Mom. She was the first of six children born to Charles Edward Layman and Lula Mae Cox-Layman in Canyon City, now Randall County, Texas. From the time Edna was born, her mother was concerned about Edna's clubfoot. In 1907, when Edna was two years old, Lula sent an ad to a Dallas newspaper asking for help to repair her daughter's clubfoot. A doctor read the item and made a long and tiring trip by horse and buggy from Dallas to Plains, perhaps thinking he was going to make a bundle of money. Actually, they had little money, but the doctor operated on the shortened ligament anyway. Edna's father held her while the doctor did the cutting. Her mother went out behind the house after saying, "If you scream, I'll come." Edna did scream as the tendon was snipped in two places, but Lula came running too late; the procedure was done. The incisions were only two small slits. The doctor measured for braces needed for many months. The first one was above the calf of her leg; each new brace was shorter. On the last one, her parents put a beautiful Sunday shoe. That doctor's efforts helped Edna walk normally for the rest of her life. The foot tired easily; she rubbed it a lot.

When Edna and Leonora were left behind to do domestic work for families, they could not attend school, and then they attended school in Socorro for such a short time before the flood. Their last school before marriage was in the rock schoolhouse at East View. Even at that school, Edna did not complete the eighth grade. She could not read, but she was excellent at mathematics. She worked in the home of Sarah and Ben Spencer for almost a year before Charles and she approached Ben to tell him they wanted to marry. Ben had observed the abilities of Edna and felt she would be the helper Charles would need in life. He went to Edna's mother and said, "Lula, if we don't allow them to get married, they will proceed anyway." Charles Spencer and Edna Mae Layman were married January 8, 1921, in Mountainair by Judge Speckman, editor of the local newspaper. Their witnesses were Mrs. Speckman and Mr. Gooseman, the typesetter. They locked the door in case Lula or Sarah came to stop the wedding. Someone knocked on the door. Mrs. Speckman went to the door. It was John, Charles's younger brother. She let him in and locked the door, and the wedding continued. After the wedding, they turned the horses toward East View. Floyd laid the reins on the edge of the wagon; the horses knew the way home. As was the family custom, they sang

"When The Work's All Done This Fall," and other songs, all the way to East View. Their first daughter, Louella Mae, was born almost two years later on October 21, 1922. I was born eighteen months later on May 3, 1924. Calvin Lee arrived on January 27, 1928. Their youngest, Royce Ray, arrived on November 24, 1932.

I could easily write a biography of my mother. She moved so many times in her life that she and I discussed naming her story, "These Old Houses," or "Edna Of The Early West." In 1937, we were living in Hot Springs (later called TorC), New Mexico. One day, she was out in the yard of the adobe house we had built as a family. A voice called to her, "Edna." She froze, as she never forgot that voice; she thought it was her father's. She turned to look, but still was not sure, so she asked, "Who are you?" "I'm your Uncle Sam Layman," a man said. She left no doubt that he was not welcome. He persisted and finally she talked with him. He had come from Earth, Texas, to bring his teenage son, L. G., for the hot mineral baths, as he was ill and in a wheelchair. Uncle Sam and his wife, Bessie, became close friends to my parents.

In 1985, I visited Louise Powers in Fresno, California. She was a friend from Albuquerque. She was aging and moved to Fresno to be near Barbara and Benny Aker, her daughter and son-in-law. While there, Louise asked me if my mother had relatives in Deaf Smith County in West Texas. At the time, I hadn't a clue where that county was. I said, "Well, Mom was born in Canyon, Texas." Louise exclaimed, "So was I!" She had known my mom in New Mexico for many years but, as usual, they had not discussed the past.

Louise continued, "I have a book, a history of that Texas County. There are people in the book who have your mother's eyes. Could she possible be related to them?"

I asked, "What is the name of the people?"

"Layman," she replied, as she brought me the book. There was Mom's Uncle Gilmer and family from Hereford. They did look like my mom.

Despite being born with a clubfoot, Edna was a fast and thorough worker; she wasted no motion. That is something I was taught in nurses' training; she seemed to be born with that ability. She might have learned it as a means of survival when she was hired out at age twelve and her mom was far away in Oregon. As we left Phoenix on the trip that led to finding her father's grave, she started crocheting an afghan. We made the long circle to Seattle, Washington, and back to Phoenix. On the day we arrived in Phoenix, Edna presented the finished afghan to her sister, Leonora, as a thank-you gift for the trip in her Honey motorhome. Edna had little money, but such as she had, she shared with love. When Edna could scarcely read, she improved her skill by reading the Bible after she became a Christian. Then a time came when Dad and Mom felt God had called them to pastor churches. Again, Mom worked hard to prepare herself. She tackled all sorts of correspondence courses on the Bible, and received many certificates for completion, so she was a good speaker on doctrine and prophecy. Dad had powerful, convincing, personal testimonies about God's power to heal and perform miracles. They became licensed to preach with the Assemblies of God and these abilities complemented one another. They sincerely wanted to help people. They loaned their car in 1946 when I transported little Martha Roberts all over New Mexico before she went to India. Through the years, as I traveled in New Mexico, I met people from churches Dad and Mom had pastored, and they related precious memories.

At times Charles and Edna went into private mom-and-pop businesses. Dad was considered the owner, but Mom put her whole strength into their efforts. She did bookkeeping and physical labor. When pastors had to be absent from their local church, they asked Edna to fill in as speaker. As a result, she had some very loyal friends in New Mexico churches. When one of their places of business was in Belen, Edna seized the opportunity to take a course at the Los Lunas Children's Hospital and Training School. She completed the course and was awarded a certificate as an attendant in the wards and cottages. It was as if she was still driven not to be without a way to make a living for her family, yet her children were grown and gone from the nest.

In the years Mom could no longer care for Dad or herself because of the Parkinson's Disease and TIAs, she lived with her children, first with me, and then with Royce, and finally with Mae. When she lived with Royce, I was helping Dad in his later years. Mom had planned all her life to go to Mae, the eldest daughter, when she could no longer care for herself. Mae had planned the same. The time came. For Christmas, 1993, Royce and I rode with Calvin and his wife, Yvonne, to De Queen, Arkansas where Mae and her husband, Dave, had been caring for Mom. Dave lovingly called her, "My mean ol' mother-in-law," to his bowling buddies. All of Edna's children were with her for Christmas and New Year's celebration. During that week, we received the phone call telling us that my Uncle Roy, Dad's youngest and last living brother, had passed away in New Mexico. We could not leave Mom even to go to Uncle Roy's funeral, as we knew Mom would not be with us long. Finally, when we did return to New Mexico, we were summoned back immediately. Edna Mae Layman-Spencer had died January 5, 1994; she was 89.

The First Family Church, my home church in Albuquerque, gave me money to fly back for the funeral. I was still almost ill from the journey by car at Christmas time. Royce and I flew to Little Rock. He was ill with influenza that whole trip. We went to pick up a rental car in Little Rock to drive to my sister's home in De Queen. The agent said, "Sorry, we do not have another Chevrolet; they have all been rented by people who are here for the funeral. Are you here for the funeral?" I said, "Yes." Then I realized I was missing something! They would not know about my mom's funeral. I asked, "What funeral?" She looked surprised and said, "President Clinton's mother; her funeral is here in Little Rock today." I was so tired, sick, and busy traveling that I had not been listening to the news. I thought, "Leave it to my mother, Edna, to go out with the President's mother!" The rental agent continued, "Will it be satisfactory if we give you a Buick as a substitute for the same price?" We agreed. It was a lovely drive to De Queen and back, but our hearts were so heavy. We had lost our mom; she had love enough for everyone.

Uncle Roy's passing meant that all of Ben Spencer's children, including the four sons of Sarah, were gone and Mom's passing meant that only one of the sons' wives still survived. Uncle John's wife, Dee Swope-Spencer, was still living. She was a sister to Linda Bratcher-Crider's mother, Bernice Swope-Bratcher-Matthews. In the 1990s, Linda became director of New Mexico District Women's Ministries, while her husband, Tommy, became secretary-treasurer of the New Mexico District Council of the Assemblies of God. My sister, Mae, and I went to Belen to visit with our Auntie Dee and to tell her that Edna had died. Of course, her children had already told her. Edna and Dee had been good friends since girlhood. Dee was aged and ailing, but she said, "I know what you are saying, and I'm gonna miss Edna." Dee lived three more months and died March 5, 1994. It was the end of an era, the end of the four sons of Sarah Adkins and Ben Spencer.

1-2. 1904 wedding of Charles E. Layman and Luella M. Cox. 3. Sara and Lorena Cox; Charles with Edna, Leonora, Jack-1910 to Canyon for Johnny's birth. 4. Group at Dixon Ranch 1907. (Circled is Charles and Lula, my grandparents.) 5. Great-grandpa and Great-grandma, David G. and Mary F. Layman in San Antonio with daughter, Molly, and son Walter in buggy. 6-7. Grandpa and Grandma, John and Sarah Cox, at Confederate Veterans Convention in Canyon, 1900. Daughter, Lorena (right) in balcony sang with Sweet Adelines. 8. Founders of Plains, Texas. 9. Leonora Layman Wister, frist baby born in Plains. 10. Gilmer and Sam families at Bronco, New Mexico.

1. Grandpa Charles Layman, Calif. 2. Mamaw Lula and my mom, Edna, at Mom's birth house, Canyon, Texas. 3. Edna before club foot repair. 4. Edna, Leonora and Jack started to school; happy! Their dad left 1916. 5. Edna and Olivia. Family moved to rock house, mud floors and two miles to mescalero school. 6-11 Grown children and companions by age: Edna Spencer, Leonora Wister, Jack L. Johnny L., Charlcie Halsworth, and Olivia Franklin. 12. Honey RV, Edna and Leonora with Don and Jean, Charles' two we found 1984. (Phone call: Jean died today, May 21, 2000.)

## CHAPTER 3

# *Charlese:*
# *Looking For the Roses*

L EAVE IT TO A professional midwife to want to know the circumstances surrounding her birth. Grandpa B. B. Spencer had been dead just over a month when I became a glint in my father's eye. As a midwife, I calculated it was July 25, Mom's birthday. Grandmother Sarah Ellen II Adkins-Spencer (Mother Spencer) was in Albuquerque with Roy, her sixteen-year-old son. He was in St. Joseph Hospital with the severely injured leg from the train accident that killed his dad on June 11, 1923. Mother Spencer's other two unmarried sons, Floyd, 23, and John, 19, were batching in Eastview. Charles, 22, was married to Edna Layman-Spencer. Life as they knew it was vanishing before their eyes.

Grandpa Layman, Edna's dad, had been gone since 1916. Where? No one knew. Grandma Lula Cox-Layman (Mamaw) was cooking at a Mountainair cafe and living in the Spencer Office Building. Four of her six children were still living with her: Jack, 14; Johnny, 13; Charlcie, 12, and Olivia, seven. Lula's two married daughters, Edna Mae Layman-Spencer and Leonora Layman-Brown, lived in the three-cornered Spencer town house next door to their mother. Edna's Louella and Leonora's Lester had been born there in October 1922. Charles and Edna chose to take Mae, their firstborn, and return to Eastview in the Manzano foothills so Edna could cook for Sarah's sons while she was with Roy.

While Charles and Edna were waiting for my birth, they were in big trouble. Food and money were almost nonexistent. With both their fathers gone and the financial depression deepening, they were catapulted into an adulthood for which no young couple could possibly be prepared. A local store was robbed just before two men left on a freight train to California. Mom said they gave her a bolt of cloth from which she made her maternity dresses and my layette and "several families got food." Someone had to be blamed, so anyone who could possibly be connected, and didn't run away, was jailed in Estancia, the county seat. Seven months into Edna's pregnancy, she was chauffeured by a lawyer to Manzano, Punta, and ranches in Torrance County to secure signatures on a bond that released her husband. She said she had only candy bars to eat on those trips, so it could be the cause of my lifetime violent allergy to chocolate. Charles, free because of the bond, went with another man to work in the wheat fields of Texas, Kansas, and Nebraska. In March, soon after he left, Edna had an attack of appendicitis and wrote to tell Charles. Dr. Buer scheduled to take young Edna on a train to Albuquerque for surgery. However, she said he was called to the Hewett ranch to deliver a baby, so they missed the train. Edna got better. When Charles received Edna's letter, he worried about her and returned to New Mexico and the court trial. I do not know what happened to others accused, but he was released, as, "He had never been accused of such before, and he had a young family to feed in the severe financial depression."

⁓

Months passed before Mother Spencer returned to Eastview from the Albuquerque hospital with her son, Roy. My parents moved back to the three-cornered house in Mountainair to await my birth. Grandma Lula Layman, who still lived next door in the office building, delivered me May 3, 1924. Doctor Buer was out of town again, delivering a baby on the east mesa. As a midwife, I've observed that the birth of a mother's second child is usually easier than the first, but in the case of my birth, it was not so. There was a large caput succedaneum, a swelling of edema caused by long labor, on my head at the time of my birth. By morning, when Dr. Buer arrived, the edema had been replaced by cephalhematomas on at least two of the cranial bones. In a difficult labor, small blood vessels break and form a clot in a pocket formed by each cranial bone and its thin covering of tissue called the periosteum. Pockets are individual and do not cross over to the next bone; it stops bleeding by building its own sealed pressure. Mom said you could see the jagged edges of each bone. It takes months for the blood to slowly absorb. The doctor was frightened because one of his children had been born a hydrocephalic and died. He said, "Edna, she is a water-head baby (hydrocephalic)." Of course, my young mother believed this; so did the doctor. I believed them until I became a registered nurse and certified midwife. The doctor left some kind of strong medicine for Mom to give me. When she traveled, she wrapped the medicine in a diaper. A bit of it leaked and the diaper turned brown and crumbled like it was burned. Was it hydrochloric acid? I don't know. I do know I had stomach problems from birth. Was it inherited, or acquired from the strong medicine? Mother never said they prayed and a miracle took place; she believed the medicine cured me. So far as I know, there is still no strong medicine in modern medical science to cure a hydrocephalic. Shunts are usually involved in draining off excess fluid. I was no hydrocephalic. The doctor was so distraught that he refused to sign my birth certificate; my Mamaw Layman signed it as midwife.

Mom and Dad stayed for some time in the three-cornered house because of my condition. They eventually, moved back to East View. They worked in the sawmill and on farms. Edna helped Mother Spencer as she had Roy to care for. The MacDonalds, Ben's partners in the sawmill before he was killed, moved in with Sarah so everyone could eat; the depression was deepening. Lula Layman got someone to take her to East View to check on the food problem. I suspect Edna wrote to her mom. Lula made noises like a mother-in-law about hungry grandchildren, and Charles asserted his authority as head of the house. As a result Dad put me, clad only in a diaper, out on a snow bank and dared Edna or Lula to go get me. Both Dad and Mom have related this story to me in their way. I survived; I'm here!

It got worse. Mom complained bitterly that there was nothing in the house to cook. Even the seed beans had been eaten; they couldn't farm without seed. Dad and Mom had their first serious disagreement. Dad had no father to depend on. The four of us got into a wagon, and Dad took us to Mountainair. In front of the three-cornered house, Dad pulled on the reins and said, "Whoa." We all got out—except Dad. What we called the three-cornered house was simply three rooms in the shape of an "L" with neither plumbing nor electricity. There was a trianglular porch where the fourth room would have been, had the house been square. The porch was about eighteen inches off the ground. Tumbleweeds totally hid that porch and a step up to it. I had my first recollection of life. The brisk March winds had piled and tangled the dried Russian thistles into heaps higher than my head. To a tiny, spindly legged, towheaded tot, this was an impossible barrier. I stood motionless, holding hands with big sister, Louella Mae, on one side and Mom on the other. We watched as Daddy Charles snapped the reins on the backs of the horses. They took off with a start. The wagon and Daddy moved down the dusty road and out of sight; I did not understand. I can only wonder what my mother was thinking and feeling. She was twenty-one years of age. Her own father, Charles Layman, had driven away just ten years before when she was eleven years old; he never returned. Her mother raised six children alone. Edna vowed not to let that happen to her children. The massive mound of tumbleweeds was no match for young Edna. She parted them, found the steps and sat me, my redheaded sister, and a suitcase on the porch. She went across the street to a friend and borrowed three dollars for train fare to Albuquerque. She retrieved us from the porch, and the friend made breakfast for us before we left. That incident was my first recollection of life. From that moment, I knew I was Elsie Charlese Spencer, a separate, living, thinking human of flesh and blood. Security flew! You could say, "It was a rude awakening."

An odd thing happened that day. While in front of the Mountainair house, I saw what seemed to be, to my right about a block away, a house with a bank of old roses on a trellis. I have tried many times to stand where I stood then and look for those roses. I could never find them. They were so real that I decided they must have been in another lifetime; I told no one. Next morning, I awoke in an Albuquerque upstairs bedroom belonging to Mrs. Davis, a friend of Mom's from the Plains, Texas, area. In spite of the bad experience of the previous day, I kept remembering that bank of wilting roses. I looked for them for years, each time I went back to Mountainair.

Mom took a job cooking for tubercular patients so she could pay Mrs. Davis for our board and room. Doctors back east were advising people who had tuberculosis to go west for the sun. The Depression caused many private homes in Albuquerque to be converted to boarding houses for tubercular persons. The Presbyterian Hospital held the most severe cases; it became a general hospital in later years. Mamaw Layman had also moved to Albuquerque and brought my teenage aunts, Olivia and Charlcie, to visit us. Mom's sister, Leonora, came from California, on her way to Mountainair to get her son, Lester. She reported to Dad that I was very skinny and might have tuberculosis. Dad came to Albuquerque near my third birthday. I remember his footsteps as he came up the stairs and that I was afraid; I clung to Mom. She was reluctant to reconcile until he got a job. He was soon employed by Gross Kelly or Breese Lumber Company. I believe it evolved into Baldridge Lumber and Hardware Company. Dad knew the lumber business from working with his father, but he loathed working for wages. Dad, Mom, Mae, and I moved in with Mamaw Lula and her two daughters in a small house in northwest Albuquerque.

In the fall of 1927, Dad bought an old Chevrolet car without a top and persuaded Edna to return to Mountainair and help him sell a load of peaches. Mae and I did not go. On the way, the car broke down near a graveyard at the village of Manzano. Someone pulled the car into Mountainair, while most of the peaches rotted. Edna found she was pregnant with their third child. She said Dad was happy, attentive, and motivated to work when they were expecting. He got a job to pile beans at the Sadler farm. Edna took in washing, although she must buy water by the barrel from the Whitehead or Perkins trucks. A long oval boiler atop rocks in the front yard boiled the white clothing, bed sheets, and other linens. Every few minutes Mother would call, "Go punch down the clothes." Once when my sister ran out to punch down the whites, she stepped on a glass lemon squeezer broken in half and slashed the bottom of her foot. Mom packed it with ashes to stop the profuse bleeding and then drove out to get Charles from his job. The car high-centered on a stump and pushed the oil pan up against the flywheel; it made a terrible racket. Mom said that was the first time she had driven alone. Dad crawled under the car to repair it while Mom told him about Mae's foot. Mountainair was still known as the pinto bean capitol of the world. Local farmers deposited their pintos in a bean elevator near the train tracks. Beans were put into one hundred-pound gunny (burlap) sacks to be freighted to far places by train. Dad took the job of sewing bean sacks shut. Mom said my sister, Mae, started school that year. My parents rented Mr. Condry's little brown house in northwest Mountainair to be near her school. My oldest brother, Calvin Lee, was born in that house on a cold January 27, 1928, when I was three and a half years old. Mae and I were sent across town to sleep at Mother Spencer's house behind the Lawson home. She had moved there just until her office building was vacated. Even she could not find food to eat in East View anymore. The bean dust at the elevator caused Dad to cough day and night. He may have had tuberculosis when he was motivated to work in the dusty bean elevator to support his growing family. (Years later, Dad was treated for secondary tuberculosis of the urinary bladder at the Presbyterian Hospital in Albuquerque.)

In the spring of 1929, just after Calvin was a year old, we moved to the Jemez Mountains so Dad could work in a sawmill. That was the trade he knew best. Mr. MacDonald, Grandpa Ben Spencer's last business partner, had taken some of their sawmill machinery, including a planer, to the Jemez Mountains. Times were hard and money was scarce, but we had a car. On our way to Jemez, it broke down in San Ysidro. Sand blew into our mouth and eyes as we helped Dad repair the car. Indians came to watch. We tried to communicate; they did not understand English. Dad tried Spanish. Everyone smiled a lot, and the car was finally repaired. Forever after, our family has referred to that town as Sandy Cedro. I do not remember a town called Jemez Springs at that time; I only remember the Jemez Pueblo. (Jemez Springs was named All-American City in 1995.) Colors of the mammoth cliffs changed around every turn.

We stopped at the Soda Dam, but turned back a bit to go to the sawmill where pine trees got taller. Dad's older brother, Floyd, was already there. We slept that night in his one-room canvas tent. It had a rough plank floor. We children and Uncle Floyd slept on the floor on pallets. A rough pine frame, filled with pine needles, served as a mattress for the one bed, where Dad and Mom slept. The next morning Mom started the wood fire and went back to bed to let the tent warm up. We awoke smelling smoke. The tent was on fire! The hot stovepipe going up through the canvas roof had ignited it. The adults were shouting; we kids were crying. We moved into a sawmill slab house where the wind blew through the cracks. We three children came down with whooping cough; it was especially hard on Calvin. Mother complained that there was no milk to buy for him and he was not yet two. Mae had nosebleeds. Uncle Floyd said it was from the high altitude; they should cut her long, curly red hair. They did, and the bouts of bleeding stopped. When autumn came we moved back to the three-cornered house in Mountainair. I looked for the roses.

There was a cafe uptown in Ruff Waldon's building. My dad developed a mastoid abscess managing a smoky back room for pool and gambling. He went alone on the train to Albuquerque where Dr. R. W. Lovelace, Sr. did surgery. There was no money for Mom to go with him. While Dad was gone, my infant cousin, Johnye Fern, took what the doctor called double pneumonia. There were no wonder drugs. Her father, John, came from the Chastain farm outside of town to get my mom and Sarah, his mom, to help take care of the baby girl. Uncle John said his wife, Dee, had been staying up night and day. John's baby improved, and Mom came home. Mother Spencer stayed longer. Mom had left her two teen-age sisters, Olivia and Charlcie, to take care of my sister, brother, and me. Aunt Olivia and my sister, Mae, got into fierce fights. When one got a frying pan, I thought someone would be injured, and I was so afraid. It had to be totally benign, as neither seems to remember. When Dad came back from mastoid surgery in Albuquerque, he walked from the train depot to the three-cornered house in a blinding blizzard. He returned to work in the closed-in, smoky pool hall and the mastoid area on the other side began to swell. Mom, always the nurse, rubbed it and applied hot packs; the swelling went away.

Mother Spencer returned from Uncle John's home to her office building next door. It had a garret, a side room for wood, and storage. Being a teacher, she had many books stored there. I loved to look at them. One was *The Wreck of the Titanic*, with pictures. At that particular time, an older man was renting just enough space in the side room for his bed. Sarah cooked meals for him. People slept and got food the best way they could. One day, a playmate and I saw them at the dining table. We ran to Mom and Dad and said, "We saw Mother Spencer sitting on the old man's lap." Mom believed us; Dad did not. They argued. I'm not sure whether it was true, but in any case, they were both single. My Mamaw Layman and my two young aunts, Olivia and Charlcie, came from Albuquerque to see us. Mom went with them to Hot Springs and took us three children with her. It was in the spring of 1930. There were seven people in that tiny car. I learned how guilt felt; I believed Mom left because of what I told them about my Grandmother Spencer. Each time Mom and Dad separated after that, I knew I had done something bad again.

The Star car crept over the south end of the Manzano Mountains past Abo and Dripping Springs and across the desert southwest to the Rio Grande River. The wheels skidded into and out of deep sandy ruts along the river past Socorro, San Marciel where Hilton's Hotel was, and San Antonio. The trip seemed unending to me. At Nogal Canyon, Mom maneuvered the car down the north rocky escarpment slowly, in a low gear and her brakes held. Going up the south side was another story. All but the driver got out to walk as the car kept threatening to roll backwards off the embankment. My teenage aunts had to scotch. That is, every time the driver made some advancement, they shoved a big rock behind the rear wheels so progress would not be lost. We were safely walking to the top with my Mamaw. Finally, we saw the lake. The Elephant Butte Dam was so new; the lake was small, but it looked vast to us.

In Hot Springs, Mom's younger brother, Johnny Coyle Layman, was working in Shelton's restaurant. We rented a small house on East Main. There was a hot mineral bath-house across the street. We three children went into the hot springs for our first time and broke out with measles. A big sign, tacked by the side of our door, notified all that we were under quarantine. We stayed about three more weeks; the quarantine was lifted, and Dad came to get us. Mamaw and her two young daughters, Olivia and Charlcie, stayed in Hot Springs with Uncle Johnny. Dad and Mom were happy; we were back in Mountainair. Calvin became seriously ill al-most immediately. A cat had scratched his hand. It seemed to be getting well, but Calvin broke out with a rash. A doctor nailed the white paper beside our door again, "Quarantined for measles" a second time within weeks. A pocket of pus formed under Calvin's arm, so Mom and Dad, in spite of the quarantine, took him to Albuquerque. He had septicemia, blood poisoning from the cat scratch, and he would have died without treatment. While we were in Hot Springs, Daf-fodil Warden, a friend my Mamaw Lula had known near Roswell, gave Calvin a snow-white sailor suit. It fit him per-fectly. He lost so much weight that after the illness, his sailor suit looked like it hung on a coat hanger. He recovered, but slowly.

Mom returned to her home laundry to contribute to fam-ily finances. She brewed beer and sold it, and friends drank it. When people came to the house to buy beer, they often gave Calvin some. Mom was not too happy, but he loved it. He held a bottle by the neck and walked around the house as he drank it. The doctor said the sugar and hops used to flavor beer might have boosted his recovery from septice-mia. When he fell out of his high chair and left a great scar on the right side of his forehead, we jokingly blamed the beer. When he was thrown against the rear-view mirror in the family car and put a matching scar on the other side, we teased that he had been dehorned! My Aunt Leonora declares that the doctor who thought I was a hydrocephalic gave mother the recipe for that beer when I was so skinny and that I also walked with a bottle in hand.

The pine and cedar trees were bathed green by rains. It was spring 1930 when we moved to Tererro in the Sangre de Cristo Mountains on the Pecos River. Massive mountains surrounded us again. The Jemez Mountains had been awesome; so were these, but different. It was a welcome wilderness; we saw deer and other animals often. Our front-yard patio furniture was planed sawmill lumber tables and benches under a tree where we ate most meals. Pet chipmunks demanded food. I had reached heaven, the top of the world! The Pecos River, rapidly losing altitude, sang with variable trills as the clear, frigid, trout-laden water rushed southward toward the town of Pecos. Our canvas tent was on the side of a hill slanting up from Cowles Ranch. It was early in the mining boom, so there was no Gifford Town yet. Inside, we had no furniture except a stove and beds, but the tent was more sophisticated than Uncle Floyd's in the Jemez Mountains. It had a floor and the sides were built up about two feet with rough lumber straight from the sawmill. The tent was stretched above that; even adults could stand up in it! We children had lumber frames, filled with pine needles and topped with quilts just like Mom's and Dad's, to sleep on. I felt proud and was amazed how my parents did all this. The mountain storms frightened me. The special sound effects of the torrential rains on the canvas roof and the loud crack of the thunder and bolts of lightning let us know we were right up in the clouds. I was terrified no matter how often it happened.

I had just had my sixth birthday when a playmate and I stole eggs from a nearby old barn at Cowles Ranch to make mud pies. Who ever heard of making pies without eggs! A woman came and talked to Mom about the missing eggs. Maybe she thought Mom used them in her pies; Mom knew nothing. I learned the feeling of dishonesty; I never did that again! One afternoon, we children were sent down a hill to return a borrowed pair of pliers to neighbors. They lived in an all-wood house; I wanted to see inside. They proudly showed us a German shepherd and her pups. When we left, the huge dog slid unseen from under their bed and followed us. Going up the hill she overtook Mae and Calvin. Snarling and growling ferociously, the dog sprang at Calvin and tore into his abdomen. The animal must have thought we had taken one of her pups. I was running ahead of Mae, who had Calvin by the hand. I raced on up the hill to tell Mom. The owners of the dog came running and went with Mom to take Calvin to the doctor. He was a little over two years old. With several stitches and time, he has only a scar and memories to show for a horribly frightening experience. I have been terrified of German shepherds since that day.

Dad's job in the mine was a problem because of his chronic bronchitis and weak lungs. He worked different shifts and went deep into the mine with his carbide lamp. I hated the smell of that light when it had to be cleaned and filled. The deep snowy winter was soon to return to this mountain. Dad would not tolerate working at such a job in the cold, so we moved back to Mountainair. The northern mountains and meadows of Torrance County were aflame with Indian paintbrushes. Mother Spencer had rented the three-cornered house for income, so my parents rented a house from Mr. Shaw a half-mile north of the grade school. Mae and I could walk to school. Mom had Mother Spencer's sewing machine and made our dresses and bloomers-to-match for school. I would be in the primary class; Mae skipped a grade and would be in the second grade. That put her two years ahead of me for the rest of our schooling. I was excited and looking forward to my first year in school. Dad and Mom had saved money while in Tererro.

Dad went back to gambling to supplement their savings. In some way, he was involved in gambling with a man at a place called the chicken ranch near the edge of town; there were no chickens. Our home with a bedroom, front room, and kitchen was impressive indeed. We soaked the walls with a mixture of creosote and kerosene to discourage bed bugs or other insects. Heavy, blue builders insulation paper was tacked over the treated walls. The tacks with shiny heads the size of a quarter were to prevent the paper from tearing through. I thought they were quite decorative. Every day, the odor got less pungent. We had a frame to view postcards of the world; it enlarged and lighted them when we looked toward a window. We had a wind-up RCA Victorolla with a fluted speaker like a scalloped bullhorn. The tubular records slipped onto a shaft. The music was nasal, guttural, screechy and beautiful. I felt happy and secure again. How little I knew!

Mamaw had given Dad and Mom a pair of goose-down pillows. Mom ordered blankets and towels from a catalog. There was a window in the north wall of the one bedroom. East of that window, Mom and Dad slept. West of that window, Mae and I slept. The foot of our beds met at that window. Calvin's single bed was in the southeast corner of the same room. A door in the southwest corner opened into the front room. Above that door was a framed picture of Grandpa Ben Spencer with his waxed handlebar mustache.

One Saturday morning, our dog started barking. Mae and I awoke and smelled smoke and cried. Calvin clung to his dog and climbed into bed with us. Dad awoke, and bypassing his pants containing the money and diamond ring from the prior night's winnings, he ran through the door into the front room. His thoughts were that Mom might be in the kitchen fighting the fire alone. Fire stopped him in the front room; the kitchen was an inferno. He fled to the front door, but the latch on the screen was too hot to touch. He backed up and sprang through the screen door, knocking it of the hinges. It burned lying flat out in the front yard. He was dazed and in his night clothing. He feared he had lost us all, including Mom. Fred Hinton, a trucker, was passing by on his way to Albuquerque. He stopped and ran to Dad asking, "Where are the children, Charley?" Dad pointed north and said, "Inside." The tall trucker ran past Dad to that north window, jammed his hands through the panes and pulled out the crossbars. I was afraid of the stranger. Big sister, Mae, pushed Calvin, still clutching his dog, through the window to the man. Then, she pushed me out. As Mae went through the window, the flames singed her red hair on the back of her head. Dad borrowed a pair of Fred Hinton's coveralls that he wore to work on his truck; they were about two times Dad's size. We three children were in our pajamas; our new school clothes burned in a tub where they were sprinkled down for ironing. When Mr. Hinton got to Albuquerque, he discovered one of his shoes was full of blood; a broken windowpane had cut him.

Mother had built a wood fire in the kitchen stove and put the flatirons on to heat. She had hired a girl to come and iron our school clothing that day. School was starting on Monday. Mom went to the barn to milk the cow. She heard a noise and thought it was the roar of a passing truck. Suddenly, she realized it was the roar of fire. Our house! As she ran, she imagined she had lost us all, including Dad. The kerosene-soaked walls fueled the fire. A whole keg of whiskey was destroyed as it fed the flames. The conflagration lasted little more than five minutes. Our smoking car was pushed to safety. A local lady kindly cooked us breakfast of biscuits, oatmeal, and "jeech." That is what Mae always called bacon; we never knew why. At the breakfast table, Mae said, "Mmmm, these biscuits sure are good." She looked at Mom and quickly added, "Even if Mother didn't make them!" We sifted ashes for days but never found the diamond ring Dad had won the night before. Our fish were found encased in molten glass. Some things were still unpacked in a storeroom detached from the house; it did not burn. Pictures were among those unburned items.

The three-cornered house was still not available, so we moved into a small, new house a few blocks west of it. My Aunt Leonora freighted an icebox to Mom filled with dishes, rugs, linens, and yard goods. Mother wrapped Mae and me in some lace panels and pretended we were posing for pictures. Since she was relatively young, she joined in our play. My fascinating, young, good-looking Uncle Jack Layman came by in a shiny sports car. He had heard about the fire. When we asked where he had been and what he had been doing, he explained that he had been working on his macaroni farm. For a time, I considered that to be an occupational option. We could not afford the house rent for long. Dad bought a small trailer to go on the 1928 Ford coupe. With the icebox, a bedroll, and everything we had collected since the fire, we drove to Hot Springs.

Uncle Johnny tried to find work for Dad, but he could not. My Mamaw Layman had already gone to Albuquerque in search of employment. We sold the trailer and icebox, tied the bedroll onto the car, and drove north. Much of the dirt road rambled along the bank of the Rio Grande River. It was frightening to me, as a child, to look out at night and see the dark rushing water by moonlight. Suddenly, Mom gasped, "Our bedroll is gone!" We turned around and drove back several miles. As we passed one car that was going toward Albuquerque, we tried to flag him down to see if he had seen our bedroll, but he sped on. Presuming that he had found our bedroll and was trying to flee with it, we turned around and followed him. About the time we caught up with him, there was a car coming from the opposite direction. The man fleeing from us forced that car off the road and the car went into a rollover. Dad stopped to see if anyone was hurt. The lone driver came out yelling and ready for combat until Dad explained it was not he who pushed him into the ditch. The man asked us to send a wrecker, which we did. Our bedroll was truly gone! Mother made most of the quilts for our pallets on the floor where we children slept.

We passed through Albuquerque and rented two rooms in an adobe house in Bernalillo, the county seat. Dad found temporary employment. Again, we three children were sleeping on a pallet on the floor in the kitchen. Calvin pointed to a huge centipede on the floor near us and yelled, "Sank, a sank!" We all screamed and crawled up on the kitchen table. Dad came to the door, thinking someone was in the kitchen with us. The critter was killed, and we went back to our pallet. Dad's temporary job ended, so we moved in with our Mama Lula at 1419 South Edith in Albuquerque. Dad left us there and went to find work. Since the fire, our schooling had been on hold. I loved to walk north on Edith to Central Avenue (Route 66). A cluster of young trees at the east edge of town identified the location of the University of New Mexico. In my wildest dreams, I could not have imagined that I would someday earn a bachelor of science in nursing from there!

One day, Mamaw Lula was driving us in a Ford coupe north on Broadway. A grassy median divided the north and south lanes. At the Grand Avenue intersection, there was a cement water fountain on the median. There were cars coming south on each side of the water fountain. Mamaw Layman went to the center and hit the fountain. It leaked for years, until the city removed it. Calvin was standing behind the seat; his head hit the roof, and he was crying. Mae was sitting between Mom and Mamaw and was not injured. I was sitting in Mom's lap. My head broke the windshield, and my face was cut in several places. The deeper cuts were on my cheeks and under my eyes, and my lower lip was cut completely through. A man in a passing car saw me crying as I sat on a curb with blood on my face and clothing. He grabbed me and put me in his car, saying, "This child is hurt." Mom gave Calvin to Mamaw and got into the car with the stranger. They took me up Grand Avenue about two blocks to St. Joseph Hospital, where they sewed up the lacerations and kept me overnight. For breakfast, they brought me bananas and cream. Talk about cruelty to children! I could not get my mouth open wide enough to eat this delicacy I had seen few times in my life, if ever. The dish and its untouched contents went back to the kitchen.

Edna was ashamed to stay with her mother permanently; she wanted Charles to make a living for their family. With her three children in tow, she walked west from South Edith across the railroad tracks to South Fourth Street. She thumbed a ride. The car that stopped had two men inside. We all got in. One man said he was a drummer. Mom said she thought he was a traveling salesman who drummed up business for his company. They let Edna out on Main Street in Belen. She searched and found Dad and his brother, Floyd, gambling in a room behind a pool hall with a man called Shorty Kelso. What a surprise she gave them! In defense of Dad, Mom said, "He was doing the thing that was most likely to bring in money for his family." Shorty Kelso admired Mom's spunk, and Dad became a bit jealous. My parents rented a room from Mr. Aragon in an adobe house in the north part of Belen. Uncle Floyd and we children were again sleeping on pallets. Mom bought a washing machine on credit and took in washing. The agitator in the modern washing machine eliminated punching down the whites! My parents eventually rented two rooms. Mae and I finally started our school year, very late, in Belen. One day, students were let out of school early because of bad weather. Mae and I were caught in a hailstorm with lightning. We got soaking wet and waited out the storm under the porch of an old hotel on North Main Street. At home, Mom washed our only white school dresses again. They were made after the fire, from contents of Aunt Leonora's icebox.

Word reached Belen that there was sawmill work in Tererro, north of Santa Fe. Dad had worked there once before, but in the deep mines. Dad, Uncle Floyd, and Shorty Kelso left to explore work and payroll possibilities. Mom stayed in Belen, where Mae and I finished the school year in the spring of 1931. When school was out, Mother's sisters, Babe and Charlcie, drove Mom and us three children to Tererro in a borrowed car. Dad was indeed working again. Mom was convinced that Dad had a steady job, so she went back to Belen, rented a 1922 Ford flatbed truck and a driver to haul her washing machine and belongings to Tererro. The old truck labored noisily up Labahada Hill south of Santa Fe. It rambled over hills and past Pecos. When it reached the muddy, narrow escarpment road going to the top of the mountain near Tererro, it stalled. The driver allowed Mom out to walk up the mountain with us three children. We watched in terror as the engine refused to inch the truck any higher. The brakes failed and the driver steered the truck backwards to the inside bank. It tipped over toward the downward bluff and our belongings poured down the escarpment. Items bounced until they stopped on tree trunks and bushes at various elevations. We hunted for missing items for days.

Until we got a tent set up to put our furniture in, we stayed in a one-room bunkhouse connected to a horse corral. In one corner was a stalagmite of second-hand chewing tobacco that cowboys had deposited. Mom cleaned it out and even scrubbed the walls. Suddenly, Dad became ill with Rocky Mountain spotted fever. Mom hired someone to take us to Albuquerque, where Dad was hospitalized. The rest of our family stayed with Aunt Flora Philip Green, where my Mother Spencer was already visiting her sister. My sister, Mae, still reminds me that while there, I poked at a wasp's nest with a stick, and they stung her instead of me. Dad was in intensive care and hallucinating for days. When Dad was released from the hospital, we returned to the top of the mountain. However, Dad was too weak to work much, and we had to get off the mountain before the deep snow came. We moved back to Mountainair. My Uncle Floyd moved in with his mom, who still lived in the office building. Yes, I looked for the roses!

This time, Dad wired the three-cornered house for electricity. A cord was dropped in the center of every room. Finally, Mom could use her electric washing machine in Mountainair. Punching down the whites seemed to be gone forever. There was still no indoor plumbing. We still had the little outhouse that got turned over at trick-or-treat time. At nights, because of the deep snows in the Manzano foothills, we had the chamber under the bed. My dad went back to gambling with friends at the chicken ranch. Sometimes, we had not a penny; sometimes, we had buckets of money under the bed. I learned this quite by accident one night when I went after the chamber.

One night, our life was shattered and changed forever. A car stopped in our yard. A man we knew helped Dad into the house. They were both covered with blood. They had come from the chicken ranch. The man said to Mom, "I did this to him." Then he got in his car and fled. Dad had been gambling with his buddies when he was hit on the head from behind with the butt of a gun. His friends forsook him and fled for fear the man would change ends of the gun and shoot; that man brought Dad home.

At first, Mom tried to clean and dress the wound on his head. When they went to bed that night, Dad kept taking her hand and touching his head while asking, "Can't you feel the bones grating one against another?" Uncle Floyd was scheduled to compete for a boxing title that evening; he had to cancel. Mom found someone to stay with us children. She and his brothers took Dad to Albuquerque to the elder Dr. Lovelace. The x-rays showed Dad's right temple area was shattered by a compressed fracture. The fracture extended from the crown down to the right ear. At various times Dr. Lovelace removed blood clots, small and larger fragments of bone, and pressure from scar tissue, and administered medication for pain control. It was the beginning of an episode that spanned years. When a fragment of bone would start to work out of the injury area, it would swell and a pocket of pus would form. Mom would start applying wet hot packs to his head. Sometimes, the bone would come out by itself. At times, Dr. Lovelace teased Mom by saying, "You have cheated me out of doing surgery again!" He thought that she was a great practical nurse. Dad was in and out of the hospital at various times. Mom was sometimes in Albuquerque with him and sometimes in Mountainair with us children, or we were all in Albuquerque. We lived in rooms, apartments, or with relatives. Mother said we moved thirteen times in one year, perhaps 1931. She was quick to take advantage of new things. She bought a mangle to iron flat items. She had an old car, and she picked up linens from Albuquerque motels on Route 66 and from rooming houses and laundered them. At one motel, a woman asked Mom to do her laundry and bring it back to her. When Mom delivered the clean clothing the woman said she had no money and asked Mom to "come back tomorrow." Mom asked for her name. She said, "Mrs. Johnny Paycheck." The next day when Mom returned, the motel room was empty. The woman may not have even known him! However, I thought of that scenario in January 1998, when the news media announced that Johnny Paycheck had an asthmatic attack while traveling cross-country on I-40 (Route 66) and was brought by ambulance to an Albuquerque hospital.

During the summer months after Dad's injury, Mae and I stayed with Uncle John and his family on the Bartell farm north of Abo. One evening, the cows did not get brought from pasture. We were among those responsible. Someone said we hid at the farm of John and Opal Matthews until we thought it was too late and someone else would have brought in the cows. The guilt must have weighed heavily in our direction. We were sent afoot or horseback to search for the cows in the dark; I was seven years old. I've always embellished the story, true or false, by saying my horse shied from a snake curled in a cactus and almost threw me. I swear I saw that snake! When school started, Mae and I went to Albuquerque to live with Mom in a small house on North

Broadway. We attended Roosevelt Primary School on the corner of Grand Avenue and North Broadway. Saint Joseph Hospital, where Dad was a patient, was three blocks east of the school on Grand Avenue. We got head lice at school. A health nurse came to visit us. Mom proudly told me the nurse complimented her for the contents of our breakfast; it was orange juice, oatmeal, and toast. Mom couldn't remember what they did for the lice.

Dad's head was healing slowly. Mother was pregnant with their last child. We moved from Albuquerque to the three-cornered house before the school year in the fall of 1932. The walk to school for Mae and me was much longer than from the house that burned. One morning, we walked in very deep snow. Even with boots, we decided it was impossible. Mae could not urge me on. A man came by and carried me to school. The teacher rubbed my painfully cold feet and those of other children as they arrived. She warmed us slowly.

Eventually, Dad got well enough to manage the poolroom in back of a cafe part-time. Mother continued to take in washing. Again, a messenger came bearing bad news. A young man, eighteen years old, had broken into the backroom where Dad worked and shot himself. He had gambled there the night before and lost his money. Dad rushed off with the police to deal with the problem. Because of the excitement, we children forgot to bring in the wood at night for cooking and heating the next day. Our wood was kept in the side-room of Mother Spencer's office building as she used the wood too. She heard us getting wood in the dark and felt sorry for her grandchildren. She brought a coal-oil (kerosene) lamp out to light our way. She, at age sixty, stepped off the fourteen-inch-high wooden porch right into a gopher hole. The burning lamp flew through the air and ignited the dry grass. Someone ran to call Mom. Mom sent us to call the doctor, and we learned that Mother Spencer had a dislocated shoulder. The doctor laid her on the floor, put his foot in the armpit, and with her hand in his he snapped the ball back into the socket. For the first time in my life, I heard my grandmother Spencer raise her voice. We then got the wood—without a light.

The excitement affected my mother; she went into labor. That brought the doctor to our house for the second time in one evening. The third room of our house was rented to an elderly man. Mae, Calvin, and I moved our pallets to his room that night. Our last sibling, Royce Ray, was born November 24, 1932, on Thanksgiving Day. About a year later, my Aunt Leonora Wister brought our cousin Robert Bruce for a visit. He had been born in Phoenix almost the same time as Royce Ray. We picnicked in the Manzano Mountains, ate fried chicken, and took pictures at a rock wall surrounding the so-called oldest apple orchard in a town called Manzano (Spanish for "apple").

1. Grade school 2. Playmates and flowers 3. Mae, Calvin, Charlese, Star car 4. Royce added 1932 on rock wall of oldest apple orchard around Manzano. 5. The same wall and trees in 1980. 6. Aunt Leonora and Robert 7. Aunt Charlcie 8. Aunt Olivia (Babe) 9. Uncle Johnny, Mamaw Lula (Cox) Layman, Uncle Jack visiting us around tar-paper house in Mountainair 10. Daddy Charles, babysitter with Royce while building tar-paper house. 11. Visitors' car. Left to right: Royce, Edna, "Sonny," "Sister," Charles, and Mae.

# CHAPTER 4

# Nine Times Nine Is Eighty-One

ONE EVENING IN 1933, Mother Spencer took Mae and me to youth services at the Assembly of God Church in Mountainair; we walked the mile. A. C. Bates and family were pastors. Young Kenzy Savage and his wife, Esther, were having youth meetings. For the few times I attended Sunday school with my Mother Spencer, my teacher was Roberta Green, a niece of the pastor. She invited me to go forward to ask Jesus into my heart and life. That was my first encounter with God; I was about eight. After church, a man drove us home in his car. Mae and I rode in the rumble seat. The moon gave the kind of light that I have since heard people describe at an encounter with the Holy Spirit. Inside the circle of the moon, I saw a coastline. A person with a fishing rod walked from the land into the water. I never told anyone, but I never forgot. I went to church very few times in the next few years. When I did go, I was reminded of the moon incident when I heard the children singing "Fishers of Men."

While Dad was recovering from the head injury, he built a new house for our family just one block east of the office building. My Uncle Roy and family were returning from Texas and needed the three-cornered house next door to the office building where Mother Spencer lived. Mom still had a home laundry and brewed beer for sale to help provide for the family. To babysit, Dad put Royce in a galvanized bucket while tarpapering the new house and putting a fence around it. We forever referred to that un-plastered house as the *tarpaper house*. We moved into the unfinished house when Royce was about eight months old. There were no partitions or ceilings, just one long east-to-west room with a front door in the south wall and a back door on the north. Dad planned to build more rooms on the north. The only bed was in the east end of that one long room. A table, chairs, and wood stove in the west end became our kitchen. A ten-gallon keg of beer was always brewing behind the stove. One of our after-school chores was to cap the bottles of beer when it was ready. Royce bounced in his child's seat, anchored by a spring to a rafter, and entertained us as we worked.

I was bored with school; life was more exciting outside the classroom. I acted out my boredom in school by drumming my fingers in rhythm on the top of my desk. The teacher would say, "Charlese, stop that." I stopped, until I forgot. She raised her voice and repeated her command. I stopped; I forgot! She said, "Charlese, if you do that again, you will stay after school." I stopped, until I forgot. I stayed after school along with several others. The teacher used a yardstick as a paddle. As I watched others being paddled, I decided, "That is not going to happen to me." When my time came, I grabbed the yardstick, broke it over my knee, and threw it. The teacher said, "Get out of here." I got! My sister, Mae, was waiting at the north entrance of the Mountainair Grade School. She asked, "Why are you not crying? Several kids came out crying." I don't think I ever explained fully. Our class had an end-of-the-year picnic west of town among the cedar trees and near the Ranger Station. We were to stick together. One classmate and I wandered off in the cedar trees, bored again. When we returned, we saw no students. We rushed across town, as we were to receive our end-of-the-term report cards to tell us whether we were promoted to a higher grade. We were frightened that the doors might be locked. What would we tell our parents if we went home without our final report card? The teacher missed us and was waiting; we got our report cards and passed.

Behind our new house, but not attached, was an old adobe house of two rooms lined up north and south. Inside were gambling tables and slot machines. Beer and beverages from the chicken ranch were purchased or consumed there. Dad said law enforcement officers from Torrance, Bernalillo, and Santa Fe counties were clients. Mom's oldest brother, who was adored by his nieces and nephews, was on parole due to a minor infraction. He was still angry about his father's leaving him at so young an age, so he lashed out at his world. A lawman in Albuquerque bragged that he had somehow been involved with my Uncle Talbert Jackson's wife, while he was in jail. For that remark, my uncle allegedly struck the officer; this broke his parole.

My Mamaw and her two sons drove over the Manzano Mountains to visit us, to see our new house, and to take family pictures. They had not yet seen tiny Royce. I was about nine years of age.

The population of early New Mexico was sparse, so the police knew my father was married to Edna in Mountainair. One evening, a posse of Torrance and Bernalillo County lawmen surrounded our house. One came to our front door on the south and asked to come in and Dad refused, but they had a paper, so he said, "If you will not bother my liquor." They promised, and they didn't mention it, even during the later court proceedings. As Dad let the policemen in the front door, my uncle went out the back door with Grandpa Ben Spencer's gun strapped to his ankle; he had come to our house unarmed. As he went around the northeast corner of our house, he met gunshots, so he retrieved the gun from his ankle and returned fire. My Grandmother Spencer said, "So many were shooting that I could see your house by light of gunfire." A young, under-age deputy was shot; he died on the way to an Albuquerque hospital. My dad had owned Grandpa Ben's gun since his death. Dad kept it under a pillow on the bed to protect his family. We never got the gun back after this incident, although we knew who had it. Perhaps they found it wherever my uncle discarded it in a field that night. Dad and my younger uncle were arrested. Mom's older brother escaped that night but had a bullet in him. He went back to Albuquerque, part of the way on the back of a cow. Someone removed the bullet in the Sandia foothills, about where Montgomery and Juan Tabo Streets meet today. Juan Tabo was a two-rut lovers' lane in those days. My injured uncle was captured later at a roadblock when he hid in the trunk of a car to leave Albuquerque; a supposed friend betrayed him.

During that shooting, my baby brother, Royce, was sleeping on the bed in the east end of the long room. Most of the shooting took place outside that east wall. Behind the bed stood a flat, padded ironing board without legs; we used it across two chairs. Also behind the bed were Mom's handmade quilts used for pallets that we three older children slept on. Those items stopped the bullets and spared Royce's life. As we made our pallets that night, spent bullets fell from holes in the quilts. More fell out as we folded the quilts next morning. We used the quilts until they wore out, in spite of patches. One bullet went through a curtain rod. We took it along each time we moved until stress completed the break. We used the ironing board with holes for years until we bought one that stood on its own legs.

Every morning, Mom sent us children to the local drug store to buy the *Albuquerque Journal.* The headlines told us when they found her brother and the outcome of the court case. Even as a child, I felt the stares of pity or contempt as we bought and carried the *Journal* back to Mom. The Sunday journey for the paper gave me a chance to see if someone shot out the town's only light above the bank door on Saturday night. I listened as people speculated on who did it. The court case about my uncle was moved to Las Cruces because policemen in Bernalillo County were involved. My dad and younger uncle were quickly cleared of all charges and released. Even the district attorney agreed that there were so many men shooting at the same time, it could never be proven who shot whom. Yet, my already broken-hearted uncle was sentenced to prison for eighty years; someone had to pay for a young deputy's death. An appeal resulted in a shorter term. We visited him in Santa Fe and always took him his favorite almond cake. He was paroled again later.

The incident was so costly that Mom took us to a charitable organization where we were fitted with school clothes. They were new, and the lady was kind, yet I felt everyone in school knew where those clothes came from. My parents felt it best to leave Mountainair because of their children. They traded the tarpaper house for cash and cows and moved family and animals to Hot Springs. I remained with Mother Spencer and had something to do with watering and feeding the remaining cows. It had been my lifelong desire to sleep on my Mother Spencer's feather mattress; I got my wish. In about a week, Dad returned alone and sent the remaining cows to Hot Springs by truck. There was no room for us, so he and I were forced to hitchhike. In one day, we walked twenty-two miles west on what is now US 60, passing the ancient city of Abo and Dripping Springs. By late evening, we headed across the flats toward Bernardo and the Rio Grande River.

Dad taught me my multiplication tables as we walked. We used them as a chant and kept beat with our steps. We got from one-times-one to nine-times-nine; I never forgot them! As we stopped in the shade of a signboard to rest, a car appeared from the east. The driver said, "We have no room, but if you think you can sit on the trunk and hang on, you are welcome." The rounded trunk slanted downward but Dad helped me hang on over the bumps and skids in the sandy, two-rut road to Socorro. The people turned west to California, so we got off. We got a ride with a salesman just south of Socorro. The car was beautiful, and we had the entire back seat. Dad said, "Well, what do you know!" I replied, "I know that nine times nine is eighty-one." I slept all the way to Hot Springs. I found my family in a rented house in the far north part of Hot Springs. It was at the bottom of a sharp little hill that drops off sharply into the town and on the west side of Date Street. They could have the cows there and sell milk and butter. In later years, Amin's Furniture Store and McDonalds fast food were north of that little sharp hill as the town grew and became Truth or Consequences.

In September, Mae and I started to school. We got tickets to a high school play. Late one evening, as we were walking to the play, I lost my ticket. I knew Dad would whip me hard. Mae went on to the play; I returned home. I walked in and said, "Dad, go get your razor strop; I lost my ticket." He was a bit amused by my strategy and said, "Well, what do you know?" I said with tears, "I think I know nine times nine is eighty-one." After a short pause in which I suffered, he said, "I suppose not getting to go to the play is punishment enough." That may have been the last successful time I used the nine-times-nine strategy to avoid a whipping. The grade school was on Date Street near the east base of water tower hill. In class, my rebellion was still surfacing. After a teacher told me several times to stop chewing gum, she walked to my side, stuck out her hand and asked for the gum. She stuck it on top of my head. She kept me after school and cut the gum out, hair and all. I went home with a bald spot. Mom was so angry that I feared for the teacher's life when she went to discuss the situation. I was never teachers' pet. She often kept us after school and paddled the palm of our hands with a ruler until we said, "Enough." Others finally said it; I would not. She usually gave me an extra hard whack and shoved me out the door.

After school was out for the summer, we moved back

to Tererro in the Sangre de Cristo Mountains. Dad needed money to feed six people; we four children were growing. Uncle Floyd, Dad's oldest brother, and my Grandmother Spencer had moved from Mountainair into a house in the new Gifford Town near the Tererro mine. Uncle Roy and his family were living in Indian Creek. They had written to Dad about a sawmill the company owned in Indian Creek, south of Tererro and just west of the Brush Ranch. We went. There was a rough, new sawmill house waiting for us, no tent this time. Dad got a job in the mines; we were cleaning carbide lamps again. Then, the job of ratchet setting at the sawmill in Indian Creek became available. As usual, there was gambling near paydays. Dad had help from local men and some from far-off places. We had money and food. Dad and other men went hunting, so we had meat.

For our first Christmas in that house, Mom sawed, glued and hammered cigar boxes into doll furniture. We had many friends. When the severe weather permitted and during the summer breaks from school, we played games like Run Sheep Run far into the night on the rocky hillsides of the canyon. We hid behind huge rocks, tree trunks, stumps, scrub oak, wild rose, or blackberry bushes. We fished and waded in crystal clear Indian Creek. We made friends with small critters, like chipmunks. At times, we had flash encounters with deer, bobcats, panthers, or bear. Young married women, who were lonesome in this isolated area, invited us into their homes to visit. They had jewelry, trinkets, pictures on the wall, and store-bought tablecloths. Anything we owned that was remotely similar to those things had burned in the house fire. I was almost a teenager, and I vowed to have those things someday. Years later when I got them, I didn't want to dust them!

Paul Holder, a minister, commuted to the little Indian Creek community from Santa Rosa, a town a few miles south. He had Sunday school in homes as people allowed. My cousin, Barbara, and I helped with a card class for the younger children. On school days, a bus transported quite a load of school-age children five miles up the mountain to the Tererro School System. When we passed Pick's Company Store, we were almost there. Miss Ellis was my sixth grade teacher. She taught diagramming of sentences and made grammar fun forever. Our bus driver was a local mother. Scuffles often broke out on the bus. My Uncle Roy's daughter, Helen, reminded me years later of a time when she and the bus driver's son fought on a return trip. She stopped the bus and ordered Helen off. Helen said that her big eleven-year-old cousin, Charlese, stood in the aisle and said, "No one is going anywhere." They did not. Any journey to and from school could be an adventure. One evening, just as we turned off the main road into Indian Creek Canyon, the driver slammed on the brakes. She stood up and said, "Everyone stay in your seat." That was like saying, "Everyone come and see." When she stepped off the bus, everyone ran to the front. There, lying across the road was a man who had shot himself in the head, and the gun was nearby. We knew him; he lived in a small slab house nearby. The driver just said it was too late to help him. She backed up and maneuvered around him.

Uncle Roy got a better job and moved his family to the new Gifford Town near Tererro. From there, my cousins could walk to the Tererro School, but it was through the pine trees and over a hill, and there was deep snow at times. My bachelor Uncle Floyd and my Mother Spencer lived a block down the street from them. This separation was serious to my cousin, Barbara, and me. We had become quite good friends. Before they moved, we sat on a huge boulder on the side of a hill and pledged that we would be Christians when we grew up. I'm not sure that I knew what a Christian was at that point. I thought my Mother Spencer was one, and she did not work away from her home. Maybe it was like an occupation. Barbara and I never mentioned this again for over forty years, until a Spencer family reunion in 1984. We had both kept our vow.

In Indian Creek, we could watch overhead, day and night, as the huge buckets of ore appeared on the north ridge of the vast mountain, crossed high overhead on a cable, and disappeared beyond the south ridge on their way to Glorietta some twenty miles south. We, along with friends, climbed up both steep sides of Indian Creek Canyon, more than once, to the scaffolding that held the huge cable. At Glorietta, the freight trains received the ore and carried it to smelters in distant states. We were told the tramway was the longest and highest in the world.

My Mamaw Lula cooked in Glorietta for the workers during its construction. For 1935–36, my mom was hired to cook for bachelors who worked in Indian Creek's sawmill, so we moved into the dwelling part of the cook shack. Mae and I had the first bedroom of our own. Our family spent one Christmas in the cook shack. Mom ordered groceries from Illfield's store in Las Vegas, sixty-five miles away. At Christmas, she ordered a dinner set of blue willow play dishes, made in Japan, for my sister and me. There was cutlery and a tiny eggbeater. For glasses, Mom saved wee pimento glasses after cooking with the contents. Mae and I agreed that whoever had a daughter first would own the dishes. Neither of us has produced a daughter. We have had some interesting times with the dishes. Usually, I had one cup and saucer, as I collected teacups. I was especially fond of the soup tureen, so I had it at times. She usually had the sugar bowl and creamer, as pitchers were her hobby. Once, the dishes disappeared. She said that I had them, I said that she had them. Suddenly, they appeared in her storeroom, up on a shelf not even in a box. One year, she brought them to me just before a Christmas. We took them, for the first time, to see how much they were worth. We did not like what we heard, so we kept them. They were pre-WWII, not Occupied Japan after WWII. What parts I have, I display each year at Christmas.

Mae graduated from the eighth grade in Tererro in 1936.

I finished the sixth grade and Calvin completed the second grade in the spring of 1936. Royce was not yet in school. Mom was proud that we had not missed one day that school year because of illness. She declared that it was because she made us gargle with Watkins' mouthwash every morning. The few times we missed school was because the snow prevented the bus from traveling the five miles from Indian Creek to Tererro. Steep hills made it a treacherous journey in winter. One afternoon on a return trip, the snow got deep and the bus stalled on a hill. The driver sent us wading the deep snow across a field to a house until the road was cleared and the bus came to get us.

When there was an emergency in our home, we were called in from playing on the hills. At one such time, Mom was taken to Albuquerque for emergency surgery. Along with that surgery, she also had the appendectomy that she had needed eleven years earlier, just before I was born. Once, Dad fell while riding the carriage he rode to set ratchets at the sawmill. It jerked and threw him, injuring his head again. This required another trip to Dr. Lovelace in Albuquerque. From then on, he was not well enough to work in the sawmill, so Mom and Dad started talking about leaving the mountain.

We cousins were especially fond of our Uncle Floyd, but he did have an alcoholic problem. When my inebriated uncle wrecked our car, he was uninjured, but my dad was injured again. As a practical joke, a single woman flirted with my bachelor Uncle Floyd by sending him a newborn kitten, still wet from birth, in a brown paper bag. It was no joke to me; I begged him for it, and he was glad to get rid of it. I raised it, feeding it with an eyedropper, and kept it warm in cloth inside a shoebox beside my bed. In the night when it got cold, it cried, and I put it in bed with me. When my parents decided to leave Indian Creek, the kitten was still small, but I took it with me. We went to spend our last night with relatives in Gifford Town. Mom, Dad, Calvin, and Royce stayed with Mother Spencer and Uncle Floyd. (My uncle would not go to church, but if we read the funnies on Sunday he would snatch the paper out of our hands and say, "You don't read that on Sunday!" We could not always tell when he was joking!) Mae and I slept in the home of Uncle Roy and Aunt Mabel up the street. We slept with cousins in one bed, some at the head and some at the foot. That night, someone else heard my kitten cry when it got cold. Next morning, I found it in the bed with us; it was dead! I cried and thought, "Well, what do you know?" Dad was not there to answer. The wee cat fit into a matchbox. We took him up a hill, dug a hole under a beautiful pine tree, and had a sad funeral.

When we left Tererro this last time, we went on an extended trip. We went north to Colorado to see the relatively new Royal Gorge Bridge at the Arkansas River and then west to Silverton and Ouray. We turned south into Arizona and went to Phoenix by way of the Grand Canyon, Petrified Forest, Oak Creek Canyon, and Sedona. I can only remember there being one small building at the Grand Canyon. We were totally alone at the Petrified Forest, but it never occurred to us to pick up any of the acres of stumps and logs. Oak Creek Canyon Road was not paved; I was terrified, but nature was dressed in its finest. There was only one store and a filling station in Sedona, but the views were truly awesome. In Phoenix, we visited Nevin and Leonora Wister and my cousins, Robert and Cathy.

I was twelve years old. I could not wait for school to start in the fall so I could write the usual essay of what I did on my summer vacation. In previous years, I had listened to reports like "I went to Grandma's farm. She has a turkey, a rooster, and a cow." Then the teacher would call on me, and I would read, "We traveled to Tererro and lived in a tent. We lived on a high mountain and had a chipmunk for a pet. He sat on our shoulder and ate wild strawberries from our hand. We saw deer, bear, and bobcat. We waded and fished in the Pecos River. My dad took us deep inside a mineshaft.

We saw fool's gold and real gold." This time, I couldn't wait to tell about the longest tramway in the world crossing Indian Creek, where we waded and fished. I could even tell about Colorado and Arizona.

On the way back to Hot Springs from Phoenix, we crossed high mountains into southwest New Mexico. From Silver City we descended into Hillsboro, the county seat of Sierra County. It was getting dark, so we decided to camp just east of that little town. It looked like rain, so we spread our bedding inside a miner's old cabin. In the night, we awoke scratching fiercely. Mom got up and lit a coal-oil lamp. The light showed our beds almost black with bed bugs. I awoke and thought, "Well, what do you know about that!" It took us months and a lot of creosote to rid our bedding and home of the pesky critters.

It is beyond me to know how and why we ended that trip on a farm up the Monticello Creek, northwest of Hot Springs, New Mexico. It was a beautiful place, but I had never lived on a farm and had no idea of the work involved. I was still twelve years of age. Dad and Mom rented a farm from Esteneslau Montoya. He lived in the town of Monticello, two miles south of the farm. Dad drove us up a road, almost completely in an arroyo bed. He turned, went through a gate, deposited us at a farmhouse, and left. He was off to gamble with one of his brothers and some professionals. They went to Las Vegas, New Mexico, and Las Vegas, Nevada, among other places. He planned to supplement our farm produce with cash. Although it seemed impossible, the Great Financial Depression was still deep. There was a two-room adobe house for us to live in. Split level! We entered the front and only door. It opened into a relatively large room with a floor of warped wood planks. In that room, we did most of our living. We cooked and ate and worked; that *was* our living. There was an eight-inch step up into the dirt-floored bedroom. A fire in the yard heated water for washing clothing — we were punching down the boiling whites again.

We ate before dawn, milked cows at daylight, and went to the fields immediately afterward. We came home for lunch and went back to the fields. There was a wagon and three horses, Shorty, Bill, and Stranger. Shorty was so calm that we could ride him, and we loved him. Bill would bite you. Stranger was smart and mean; he would bite, kick, or try to dump anything he was hauling. He kicked my brother Calvin in the head once; he was unconscious for a time. Bill and Stranger could pull a plow alone or the wagon as a team. I wondered, "Where did Mom learn to harness horses to a wagon or a plow?"

It was late spring when we arrived at Monticello. People said that we were too late to plant; the produce would never mature. We had to plant quickly and not waste a drop of irrigation water when the gates were opened for our share. We planted corn, chili, sorghum cane, cantaloupes, watermelons, beans, pumpkins, and alfalfa. The trees in the orchard were apple, plum, peach, apricot, and pear. One apple tree surely must have come from the Garden of Eden; it produced apples the size of grapefruit. As you ate them, you found sweet, bite-sized chunks that peeled out and tasted like pineapple; I've never seen that sort of apple again. As soon as plants were visible in our fields, we went to pull weeds day after day, hour after hour. We even kept the weeds out of the alfalfa field and fruit orchard. People of the valley stopped to ask, "How do you keep the fields so free of weeds?" Mom either had more kids, eight hands among us, or we worked harder, all by hand and hoe. Mom worked as hard as we did. Mae, as always, was Mom's right hand; she made us do what Mom assigned. Calvin and I just worked. Royce was a bit over three years of age, too young to do much work. He kept us laughing; what a joy he was. He hated clothing; he could never see the use of it. In a way he was right, as we had few visitors and it took time to keep clean. His vocabulary was curses. When we laughed, he cursed more. Was he angry because Dad left? I know I was.

The house, horse corral, and grazing land for animals were on one side of the arroyo bed, and the farm and orchard were on the other side. We were *told* about arroyos. We were not *educated* about arroyos until we saw water come down from draining the San Mateo and Black Range Mountains. Mrs. Montoya, a sister-in-law to our landlord, and her family lived straight up on top of a bluff behind our house. She said about the arroyo, "You will know when one is coming." She was right! One day, a car drove into our yard. A man and his wife were just traveling and came upon this beautiful farm valley. We visited, and they went on their way, out the gate, up the road in the arroyo bed. We never saw them again.

Soon after we went to work in the field, we heard a strange noise like a moan far away, or like people chanting. It got louder and louder. Then Mrs. Montoya's son, Little Joe, came running across into our field all excited. He said, "Come across the arroyo! The water is coming, and you will not get to your house to sleep tonight!" We ran across the dry creek bed with him and waited inside our gate. It had not rained where we were! The moaning got louder, and we asked Little Joe, "What are they saying?" He said, "Listen! *Hay viene el arroyo!* As soon as a person hears the water away up the canyon near the mountain, someone starts calling. The people who hear them take up the chant, and it is passed for miles down the mountain." It becomes a life or death call. When you hear it, you might have time to get your wagon or car out of the creek bed onto higher ground. We heard the sound many times that summer and just barely beat the headwater across so we did not have to sleep in our farm. The chant became familiar; we automatically joined in. We did not wait long that first day! A head of water, over five feet high, came rolling down a dry creek bed tossing trees with roots attached, cows, other animals, and a car end-over-end. In 1936, most cars looked much the same; we wondered if that car belonged to our morning visitors. Many years later, when Mom and Dad were living in TorC, Little Joe let them know when his mother died, and they attended her funeral. Soon after that, Little Joe was brutally murdered. The local TorC paper reported that aliens he employed might have done it for guns and money.

Our crops along Monticello Creek were beautiful. Neighbors to the north had pigs that kept breaking into our fields. Mom sent them a message saying, "Keep your pigs out of my fields." The pigs came back. Mom wrote them a note and said, "If you don't keep your pigs out of my fields, I will kill them." They wrote back, "You kill 'em; we'll eat 'em." Mom wrote them back, "I kill 'em; I eat 'em." The pigs were gone for a while, but then one came back. Mom shot it; we ate it. The pigs stopped coming.

President Roosevelt was having cattle slaughtered. The cows were not to be bought or sold because the government was paying the owners. We went to one of the slaughters. They said Mom could pick out the two she wanted, and they would kill them for her. She did, and I have never seen so much meat before nor since in my lifetime. We made mincemeat that filled Mother Spencer's crock butter-churn. We made jerky. We put heavy pepper on meat and dried it on our housetop and clothesline. The taste was fantastic! Mom ordered a sealer, and we canned great hunks of meat. Dad returned in the very late summer and helped with the harvest. We spent our time harvesting and preserving produce. One day as we picked fruit in the orchard, a centipede got up a leg of Dad's pants and stung him. He was either allergic to it or it gave a mighty dose of poison, because within a half-hour, Dad fainted. We called Mom, she took him to the house, and we continued to pick fruit. Dad was still not well from the head injury.

We canned the fruit and vegetables in tin cans and jars. We pickled beets and cucumbers. We made chow-chow and all kinds of relishes and pickles. We made jams and jellies. We dried fruit. We chewed sweet sugar cane and took some to a place where they had a press. A horse went round and round to turn the press and produce the juice. There was a huge vat where the juice was cooked down into sorghum syrup. We poured it into Mary Jane Syrup buckets to take it home. Today, sorghum is mostly used as an ingredient in cookies. Mom's freshly deep-fried sopapillas with sorghum syrup was the ultimate treat. I have read that sopapillas originated in New Mexico. My Mamaw Layman and Mom surely helped promote them. Although Dad did not make us work as hard, he was not always as patient as Mom. One day, Dad, Calvin, and I were near the horse corral between our house and our front gate. We looked up, and the gate was open. Our cows were slowly meandering down the arroyo bed, munching as they went. Dad asked who had left the gate open. Calvin and I denied guilt. Dad was so angry! He took a horsewhip off the corral fence and beat us with it. We dared not run or he would whip us later *for running*. We rolled on the ground to avoid the licks. I felt that by whipping me he called me a liar; that broke my heart. I remember thinking, "Can I ask you if you left the gate open? Can I beat you, thus calling you a liar?" Calvin and I did not usually assert ourselves verbally, but *we thought!* I could tell Dad was in no mood for *nine-times-nine*!

When fall 1936 came, it was time to go to school. I enrolled in the seventh grade. We rode our horse, Shorty, bareback the two miles to school every day and tied him to a tree. Other children did this; water was available. One morning, Shorty stumbled in the deep sand in the arroyo bed, and we all slid off over his head. He stopped, turned around, and looked at us, totally confused—like, "What are you doing down there?" We got back on and went to school. By now, so much had happened on the farm, I forgot that I wanted to write about what I did in the summer. My whole world had changed, and that tramway seemed a lifetime away. When the teacher asked me a question, I shrugged my shoulders and said, "I don't know." I did this even if I knew. I was so nearsighted that I could not tell what the teacher was writing on the board. She put me in a front row seat; I still could not see and didn't care. I could not project my anger on my parents, so the teacher got it. Another reason I was angry was because Mom and Dad were talking of moving again. We had attended school one month. It was time to receive a report card. Mae and Calvin took their cards home to Mom and Dad. They thought it was odd that I never received one. Our books were provided by the state. I had stuck my straight-F report card in one of those books and returned it to my teacher when we left.

Mom and Dad did not want to farm another year. They took all their beef, pork, cans, jars, and the crock of mincemeat and moved to Lockney's sawmill up in the beautiful Black Range Mountains west of Monticello. Dad was to work in the sawmill, and the owner of the sawmill needed more children in the one-room schoolhouse; otherwise the state was going to close it. By then we owned several cows. Dad *gave* each of us a cow of our own. We had Crump, Bossy, and Bosefus, among others. Mae's cow was Nancy, and mine was Cherry. We took turns driving the cows to Squaw Creek Canyon for water. When it was my day, I loved it. I would be alone for at least two hours. As the cows grazed, I sat on a big rock or a tree stump. Among the pine trees, I would think and listen to the amazing peace and silence. When there was a gentle breeze and organ music played in the tall pines, I imagined the angels were playing and singing. At times, snow was deep and winter became fierce in the mountains. In the little one-room schoolhouse there was a pot bellied wood stove. As soon as we got to school each morning we were told, "Go collect fire wood; then you can warm." We were so cold that we wanted to warm first. We told Dad and Mom about it. They felt Mr. Lockney had not kept his word about the work available, so they said, "Tell the teacher that she must let you warm first from your long trip to school and then you can bring in the wood." We told her, but she did not agree. Mom and Dad said, "Well, tell her you collected wood at home last night, and if you cannot warm by her stove, then you will go home and get warm." We told her; she said, "Go." We went. We have always said, "We got expelled from school." When we related the incident to our parents, Dad said, "Well, what do you know about that?" I knew by the sound of his voice it was safe to say, "Nine times nine is eighty-one." I never knew whether the school closed for lack of students or not.

It was nearing spring. Dad took Calvin, afoot, and started herding the cows east toward Hot Springs. Calvin was nine years old and needed to learn his multiplication tables. Dad taught them to him on that cattle drive. The trip became long and tiresome. Calvin's shoes totally wore out, and he was barefoot. Dad wrapped his feet. By the time they got to nine-times-nine, Dad stopped at the Alexander Ranch and traded some of the cows for two lots in Hot Springs. The rancher hauled my dad, my brother, and the rest of the cows to Hot Springs to those lots Dad bought *in an arroyo bed* in Northeast Hot Springs. We were landowners again. Dad came back to Lockney's sawmill and got the rest of us, and we moved into the Lard house up on the side of the water tower hill in Hot Springs. Mom always cleaned so thoroughly everywhere we lived. As she was cleaning that place she found a roll of paper money stuffed into the leg of the stove. We were there only until the weather got warm enough to move onto our own lots in northwest Hot Springs. At first, Dad built a simple lumber frame about twice as big as a full-sized bed. It was tall enough to stand up in. Mom sewed unbleached cotton muslin into sides and a top for it. All our earthly possessions were piled into it. If it had rained, we would have been in trouble.

Mom went to work sewing at the WPA. Mae got a job in a youth project working in the office of Mr. Sides, the primary school principal. I was washing clothing, including denim jeans, for our family of six on a rub board out in the sandy arroyo-bed yard and *punching down the boiling whites again.* Dad was doing most of the cooking since Mom worked away from home. That is where I learned Dad could make the best (pinto bean) pumpkin pies. He mashed the beans and strained them, and then added eggs, milk, sugar, and spices. He poured the mixture into a pie shell and cooked it in a coal-oil oven. Delicious!

Dad, my young brothers, and I hauled water and made adobe bricks to build a house. An insurance agent parked on a hill some distance away and spied on Dad to see what kind of work he was able to do. He had been receiving seventeen dollars per month since he left the company in Tererro. He lost his compensation by building that house for his family. The pain in Dad's head was severe and increasing. He and Mom went on a 150-mile trip north to Albuquerque to Dr. Lovelace, Sr. again. He said, "The increasing scar tissue is causing the pressure and pain and will continue to increase. You may have seizures and become more incapacitated, physically and mentally, before you die."

The whole family finally got the double garage built, and we moved in. We could now build the house! In reality, Dad had to find work to help feed the family. He bought a truck. We went down along the Rio Grande and cut mesquite wood to sell. We still had cows to be herded by one or another of us children, mostly by Calvin. Royce was entering the work force a bit. The cows were herded up the sandy arroyo beds and on the steep hills north and west of our house. The land was virgin; we encountered scorpions, lizards, rattlesnakes, horned toads, and rabbits. Some of those were in our own yard! We explored and brought home fossils in rocks. The University of New Mexico eventually sent students to digs on that very land. The transcontinental Interstate 25, that runs north and south from Canada to Mexico, now covers part of the land where we herded the cows.

# CHAPTER 5

## Hot Springs (Truth or Consequences), New Mexico, and Fort Worth, Texas

A S SOON AS POSSIBLE, we three older children were en-rolled in Hot Springs Schools to complete the spring 1937 school term. This was the fourth school for that year: Tererro, where we finished one term; Monticello, where we started this term; Lockney's Sawmill, where we were ex-pelled for not carrying wood; and finally Hot Springs. Con-struction was being done at the grade school on Date Street, so for that year, the seventh and eighth grades were moved to the high school building north of the city water tower, where my sister, Mae, was a freshman. As for me, I was one angry child, or a normal teen-ager. I lashed out where I could, since I knew I couldn't do it at home; I knew they would beat me. I tried the shoulder shrugging when the teacher asked me a question. This teacher also learned that I could not see, so again I was put in a front seat. I do not remember her name; I didn't care. A group of also-angry classmates sort of inhaled me. We harassed straight students on the way home from school. We never injured; just frightened them. For a simple reason, we'd tell them, "You did not invite us to a certain birthday party." We probably would not have gone if they had asked. When someone reported us, we were taken one at a time to the principal. He asked me about the report and then asked the teacher about my grades. She said, "Well, she cannot see, so they are bad." She never said that I was rude and did not seem to care. The principal asked if my parents had money for glasses. I said, "No." I did not tell him that my father had emphatically said, "Glasses are not for kids!" The principal said, "Make an appointment with Social Welfare and see if glasses will help." I was only warned about the truant actions. When I got the glasses, I was surprised at what was being written on the blackboard. I did not take the glasses home; I hid them at school. From what my dad had verbalized, I feared that he would beat me if I got glasses. When my grades improved, I told Mom about the glasses. She told Dad; he and I never discussed them.

Late one evening, Mae and I were walking home from a high school function. We were aware that a man had been following us on the lighted streets for some time after we left the high school. We thought the man would eventually stop off at some house; he did not. When we walked faster, he did the same. We stopped once and asked him if he would mind walking ahead; he ran ahead. Our adobe house was the last house in northwest Hot Springs. The last quarter-mile was isolated and required wading a sandy arroyo bed through scrub mesquite bushes. When we got into the arroyo, he came out of the mesquite bushes. He grabbed my sister, Mae, and told her exactly what he wanted. She had worn a pair of walking shoes, but had a pair of high-heeled shoes in a paper sack to wear at the high school. Somehow, I got those shoes and tried to give her one. I do not know how much she used the one heel, but I gave him all the strength I had with the other shoe. During the wrestling, I recognized him. I was aiming for his face with the high heels. He hesitated a moment and I said, calling his name, "Now, Mr. Jones (not his name), have you had enough? If we killed you, it would not be the first one!" The fact that I called his name may have surprised him. Perhaps he'd just had enough of the shoes; he ran away! Mae's nose was bleeding. She told me later that she was tiring. He had concentrated on her, possibly because I *might* recognize him. We went straight home and told Mom and Dad. The next day, they reported it. A policeman went to talk to the man and then came to talk with us. He said, "From the looks of his face, he will not be trying it again soon."

In school, I was gradually making friends with another student, aside from the also-angry group. Her name was Mabel Ruth Wallace. She seemed to be intrigued by the stories I told about tramways, mines, and being expelled from school. I was interested to learn that she was born at Tennie, the general area of Billy The Kid stories. We giggled a lot like normal teenagers. Now and then, she would say something about her church. One day, she invited me to go to a church meeting they were having in downtown Hot Springs. She said a minister was moving his big tent from Polvadera, north of Socorro, to Hot Springs. When I asked his name, she said, "Paul Holder." I recognized his name as being the preacher who had held Sunday school in Indian Creek homes, so I told Dad and Mom. When the minister arrived, he visited our home. My parents decided to attend the meeting once out of respect.

What are the odds of these three elements meeting? One, my grandmother in Mountainair was praying for us and attended the same church denomination that was sponsoring this tent meeting. Two, a preacher in Tererro was of that same doctrine and came to Hot Springs where we settled after bouncing around to Monticello and Lockney's. Three, a schoolgirl we never heard of would ask me, a truant, to go to a meeting that would link those factors and lead our family to help from God. Hertha Magness, a never-married lady, invited me to go forward and invite Christ to come into my heart and life. I believe our whole family became born-again Christians during that month. Mom received the baptism of the Holy Spirit at home; she awoke in the night speaking in another language. She had never seen anyone experience this. Dad received that experience under the tent. He also claimed healing for his injured head and had a vibrant testimony. This was all so new to our family, but the minister read about it from the Bible, and people claimed to have experienced it. My teenage school friend, Mabel, and I had the life-changing experience on the same evening. This was the first thing that gave us something mutual to talk about.

Being Pentecostal, or even charismatic, was not the cool thing to do in 1937. We literally went from the ridiculous to the sublime. Our family lost some friends, but gained others for a lifetime. Some relatives distanced themselves from us; others welcomed the change. The course of history in our family was changed forever. We knew no generation gap; Mom and Dad were in their 30s. Our activities together changed, increased, and became fun. There were Spencer family picnics around Hillsboro, high in the Black Range Mountains toward Silver City, and at Elephant Butte Lake northeast of the dam. We hunted for agates on the hills east of Elephant Butte toward Engle and for piñon nuts all over New Mexico. We hunted for deer during legal seasons and for rabbits for meat at any time. There were youth meetings, dinners on the ground at church, dinners with friends in homes, and the usual birthday parties with cake. When we had a bit more money, ice cream was added. We had an ice cream freezer, which held ice around a cylinder full of Mom's rich mix of our own hen eggs and cow's milk. It had a handle that must be turned slowly for almost an hour. We all helped turn the handle, but Calvin became the official turner, for he had a motive. He helped Mom dish up ice cream until the rotating paddle inside must be removed to reach the rest of the ice cream. The paddle, laden with ice cream, was placed on a platter. We all sneaked a bite, but Royce says it grew to belong to big brother. What happened to the rest of the ice cream was of little concern to Calvin!

There were fellowship meetings in churches at Deming, Lordsburg, and Silver City. We met other Christian young people in southern New Mexico. We learned that Reverend White, pastor at Lordsburg, was the presbyter of the section. His daughter, Jessie Nell (Mrs. John) Smith, still lives there. The George Pennington family lived in Silver City. The first I heard of them, he had bought a place called Cottage Sans near Silver City to have church. It had been used for health purposes, but was ideal for conventions. We attended both youth and adult camps there. The Pennington family eventually had a dry goods store in Silver City. They have always been supportive of the local churches and missions. Members of his family still attend the Harvest Fellowship Church. The Pennington's daughter, Ann, married Curtis Maxwell. The Maxwell family once lived at Cliff, a nearby town, but moved into Silver City for employment. Norma (Maxwell) Wilson was a sister to Curtis. (Her husband died when their youngest boy was two years old.) Mrs. Maxwell, the mother of Curtis and Norma, was a sister to Ollie (Mrs. Mack) Thompson in the Hot Springs church. The Thompson and Spencer families were close friends. We were especially good friends to the older Thompson children, Edythe, Annie Mae, Billy, and Francis; Lois, Lynn, and David were much younger. Norma (Maxwell) Wilson and a friend of mine, Ruth Savage, both told me that in Edythe's later years she asked for credentials with NMDC and helped to keep the Cliff Assembly viable until the day she died. Annie Mae Thompson married and lived in Albuquerque. I talked with her by phone just before she died. Billy married and moved to another state; my brother, Calvin, has visited them. A Watkins family also came from the Cliff-Mule Creek area to NMDC functions, like the annual Mountainair Camp Meetings.

Word traveled north to Mountainair and other towns in New Mexico that Charles Spencer and his family had gotten religion, *been born again.* Charles quit gambling. Edna put in a home bakery, changing the use of yeast *from brew to bread*! Some previous friends were extremely happy. People came to visit; they had to see for themselves. It made a great difference in our home. One isolated change would not have been so important, but it was the change in the over-all picture of our lives. Dad laid his cigarettes up on the top of the medicine cabinet one night and never smoked again. That church discouraged the use of tobacco, caffeine, and alcohol, saying: "Your body is the temple of the Holy Ghost, and some things are not good to put into it." Even medical science has evolved to agree with the dangers of those substances. We started thanking God for our food at meals. My parents started having a time of prayer each morning and night with Bible reading for the whole family. By this time, I had stopped seeing the old gang members and church was my life, not by force; I had found a friend named Jesus. My friend, Mabel and I could talk about Him now and not "who shot Billy the Kid." Just for fun, we got on the boys ball team. It was not long before we started talking about going to Africa and so far, I had never seen a real missionary. Church attendance three times a week became our life.

August 1937 was camp meeting time at the Assemblies of God Church on North Second Street in Albuquerque where the W. A. Vanzants were pastoring. Several from Hot Springs attended. Mom and Dad went in a flatbed truck with side rails. Several teenagers, including Mabel Wallace and Sally Mae Long, went with us. We younger ones rode in the open back of the truck, where the wind burned our cheeks and made a deafening roar. We did not mind; we had been Christians only three months. Camp was new and exciting. P. D. Holder, the evangelist from the Hot Springs meeting, attended. He wrote in my autograph book, "Camp time, long to be remembered. Just keep pressing on; don't look back. Somewhere down the line, you will have to attack things the devil will try to put on you." Ernest Mathews from Mountainair wrote, "Dear Charlese, the Bible says we must be Holy before the Lord. Be sure to do this, and the devil will never be able to bring you down. Yours in Jesus." Aileen Mathews, Ernest's sister, who died young, wrote: "Dear Charlese, It is with pleasure I write. I hope you will always remember me as a friend. Be a true Christian. Lovingly. AM at Camp." Pauline Mathews, and others, wrote admonitions. We were involved in a wreck while at Albuquerque Camp Meeting. A vehicle hit us broadside and lifted our truck up as if they were going under us. No one was hurt. Sally Mae wrote in my diary that it happened on Friday the Thirteenth. After camp, we returned to Hot Springs in the open truck; we were *happy campers!*

Construction was completed on the Hot Springs Elementary School building on Date Street, so my eighth grade class was moved back there. That year Mabel and I played softball on the boys' team. We would talk about them in their presence, using code names, so they would never know. In the evenings after school, Mabel and I would go over a hill from our house and join in practice with some of our team. That is when I learned how really ill Mabel was. She would need to stop and rest several times before we got up a hill. They let me play because I was good. At her turn up to bat, she would hit the ball and a boy would run the bases for her. Several of the boys liked her; she didn't seem to know that. We just had fun. In my autograph book she wrote, "Remember the Bible, its stories of old, remember the night God saved your soul. Don't forget our good times and even when we were turned sideways in Albuquerque. Remember our softball team by code names: Coffee, Run-Johnny-Run, Oh-dear, Papa-too, and Afterwhile. Charlese, I have found you to be a true friend and my prayer is that you will continue to live for God and prove a blessing to others. MW (14)." Other classmates who wrote in my autograph book were Ada Cory, Martha Amin, Bobby Hornbeck, Betty Washington, Papa-Too (He did not sign, so I wrote in his code name.), Evelyn Coker, Cecilia and Eddie Apodaca, Elizabeth and Grace Smallwood, Eillene Holden, Ethel Heffernan, and Helen Frost.

After my sister, Mae, no longer worked for Principal R. F. Sides, I worked for him. In 1938 he wrote in my diary, "It has been a pleasure to have you as a student. I hope that in future years you may feel your stay in Hot Springs Elementary School was a helpful event." Some other teachers who autographed my book were Mrs. Stillwaugh (English and Art), C. Woodrow (Music), and Gale Harte. My Mamaw Layman bought me a blue taffeta dress for my eighth grade graduation because she had bought Mae's two years earlier in Tererro. Mr. J. K. Reid was our eighth grade class sponsor. In my diary he wrote, "Charlese: You should try to be just a little more forward. Because of your age, you have let your classmates impose on you. I know from your hair color you have the powers of leadership; develop them. It's been pleasant to teach you."

In 1938, my Dad got the job of operating the engines that supplied lights and heat at the new Carrie Tingley Hospital for Crippled Children in Hot Springs. His years of helping his father provide power for their sawmills trained him for this position that he held four years. Also in 1938, my youngest brother, Royce, started his elementary education. He and Calvin were down at the Date Street Elementary School. Mae was a junior and I was a freshman back in the high school building north of the water tower hill where I had spent my seventh grade. I had discovered that I loved math, so my name soon appeared on the honor roll for algebra and geometry. Our math teacher gave us a problem to work on over a weekend. I worked and worked on it, and then went to bed and dreamed how to solve it. Monday morning I was asked to *put it on the blackboard*. I had come a long way, baby!

The family of my school chum, Mabel, called her Tommy. Her father was Tom Wallace; her mother was Etta. Her younger sister was Annelle. For the first two years after I met Mabel, her father worked as a cowboy on a ranch near Engle, east of Elephant Butte Dam. Etta, Mabel, and Annelle lived at the ranch with Tom in the summers when school was out. I sometimes stayed with them. My mother and my sister, Mae, worked in Engle. They worked for Leland and Polly Larson, managers of the Diamond A Land and Cattle Company. Mother organized a Sunday school in Engle. Mabel and I had children's church under a tree near the ranch where her dad and mom lived. The Gideons gave us Bibles to give to the children. Two little sisters attended. One had heart damage from having rheumatic fever earlier. After school started, that child was hospitalized in Hot Springs. She asked her mother to bring her Gideon Bible. Mabel and I visited her and prayed with her in the hospital just before she died.

⌒

Our teenaged friends in the Hot Springs church were from families named Thompson, Hilliard, Magness, Ballard, Wallace, Adams, and others. We usually did something in a group on Sunday. Once, we climbed to the top of Turtle Back Mountain after Sunday School. None of us was able to walk enough to go to church that evening. We nursed sore muscles all the next week in school. If we went for a drive, Jack Adams was the chauffeur. If the car engine died, Jack would say, "If my dad were here he would cuss this thing and it would start." We prayed a lot for Jack. He once drove his car as close to the edge of a hill overlooking the Elephant Butte Lake as he possibly could without going over. Another time, he drove the car onto the runway of the Hot Springs Airport. We opened the two front doors for wings and Jack took off down the runway to see if the car would fly. His brother, Tom, whom we called the information burro, could tell us anything we wanted to know about the Elephant Butte or Caballo dams and lakes, or how anything local got its name. He died of spinal meningitis in a CC Camp in Arizona. We mourned him, as he was a viable member of our youth group.

While we were freshmen in high school, Mabel's dad, Tom, died of tetanus gotten at the ranch. With what we know today about tetanus and the treatment, he might have survived. Mabel was also growing weaker from a heart damaged in childhood by rheumatic fever. We were forced to stop playing softball on the boys' team. After church on Sundays, I sometimes went home with Mabel's family for lunch. Her mom always made our favorite dessert, banana pudding; she made the best. When Mabel could not walk much any more, we strung cord through a doorway and ran it through chair arms in two different rooms, making it a circle, sort of like a tramway. We could not see each other but wrote notes that made us giggle about our code-named baseball buddies. We pinned the notes onto the string and ran the messages to the one in the next room. That is how Mabel announced the birth of her first nephew, Melvin, to me. He was the son of her sister and husband, Elsie and Alvin Carl, in Carrizozo. Television did not exist; we entertained ourselves. We wrote a skit about missions. (See copy in the Appendix.) We learned to chord on Mabel's guitar, so we could occasionally sing in church, but usually ended up giggling before the song was completed. My sister, Mae, had a guitar; Vivian Ballard (Rushing) had a mandolin; Mabel had a guitar; I had an accordion. When they went home with us on Sundays, we chorded and sang. They could not get enough of my mom's fresh light bread. Mom's home bakery was well known. My brother, Calvin, sold bread from a box strapped to his bicycle; everyone in Hot Springs was his friend.

My sister, Mae, graduated from Hot Springs High School in the spring of 1940. That fall, I was a junior. It was a weird feeling to be in school without my sister. She took a civil service examination in Las Cruces, and while waiting for the results, held a job with Frito-Lay in Hot Springs. Financial situations were improving a bit each year. It was still hard for pastors to receive enough tithes and offerings to eat. My parents shared their food with pastors (Powers, Vale, Largin, Rich, Walker, and others) and their families. Pastor and Mrs. Rich even stayed in our home as our companions when Mom and Dad went on a trip. My parents left with a trailer load of huge, beautiful tomatoes that grew in the Rio Grande Valley. They planned to take them to Tererro, where people had money. Before they got halfway, the trailer hitch broke and dumped the tomatoes. They returned with what tomatoes they could salvage. We ate tomatoes, canned tomatoes, made catsup, sold some and gave some away. My diary for days said our evening meal was "lettuce and tomato sandwiches with iced chocolate drink." I must have enjoyed eating it; I wrote it so many times!

Mabel and I often discussed becoming missionaries to Africa, even before we ever met a missionary. Then, Homer Goodwin from West Texas visited the Hot Springs church. He and Thelma were missionaries to the Gold Coast (now Ghana), West Africa. My sister, Mae, was secretary-treasurer of our church when we pledged one dollar a month to help the Goodwins. We had bake sales and other projects to get that much money together every month in 1939. One night, I dreamed Mabel and I were feeding sheep from a basket. Finally she said, "You will have to finish the job; I must leave." The basket was empty! There were more sheep to feed. As I awoke, I was digging so hard into the empty basket that it seemed that the ends of my fingers would bleed. In 1940, the people in the town of Hot Springs collected money to send Mabel to Albuquerque for medical help. Mr. Adams drove the car that took Etta, Annelle, Mabel, and my mom there for help. There was no treatment, even in Albuquerque. Mabel would have been a perfect candidate for a heart transplant. On October 16, 1940, Mabel Ruth (Tommy) Wallace died at age sixteen years. Her junior class of Hot Springs High school went in a group to her funeral. Classmates carried the casket. She was a popular and talented girl. She played the guitar at school and church. Her artwork, as a high school student, was displayed in an art show in Albuquerque. After

Mabel died, I wrote this poem:

### Jesus, and My Pal

*Will you let me tell you something,*
*That my heart has longed to tell,*
*Ever since my teen-pal left us,*
*To heed the call of God's great bell?*

*I have been so very lonesome,*
*How I miss her every day.*
*Four short years we were together,*
*In God's service our young way.*

*Many times I'd lie and whisper,*
*"Why Lord? Oh, why was it not me?*
*Why did not you take me, Jesus?*
*She was talented for Thee."*

*Oh, my friend, if you have lost one*
*Who shared your days through bad and best,*
*You know the feeling that was in me*
*When they laid her form to rest.*

*I suppose I had wrong feelings,*
*Of her early-setting sun.*
*Then I prayed and got the victory,*
*'Not my will, but Thine be done.'*

*Now I have one goal before me,*
*And to win, I'll forfeit all.*
*To be ready when He calls me.*
*Then meet Jesus, and my pal.*

Through the years, since Mabel left us, Etta, Annelle, Elsie, and their families have remained a part of my family. I added a note to the poem when I realized that some of our group from Hot Springs was not holding onto their faith. That in no way means that Mabel would have gone astray. It only means that any of us could. I wrote:

*Years have gone by and I see why He took her.*
*We best sacrifice body than let the soul suffer.*
*The pleasures of life, they glimmer and gleam.*
*Young people don't try them; they aren't what they seem.*

—CS 1951

For months, Dad found a ride or walked a mile over rocky and sandy hills to his work at Carrie Tingley Hospital. Then my parents sold cows and bought a 1933 Ford, and I learned more about the value of baling wire by helping Dad work on another old vehicle. We decided to go to Mountainair before school started to bring Mother Spencer to Hot Springs for a visit. Dad and Mae were working so Mom drove the car. I sat in front with Mom; Calvin and Royce rode in the back seat. By the time we got to Bernardo, darkness had fallen. Signs of roadwork were evident; US Highway 60 was being paved for the first time from Bernardo to Mountainair. At Abo, very near the place where my grandfather Spencer was killed by the train, Mom hit an unlit pile of gravel, which spun the car completely around and dropped us off between two guard posts into a small canyon with an arroyo bed in the bottom. When the car stopped rolling, the lights were still on and the horn was honking. Mom crawled out, went up on the highway and began walking up and down, wringing her hands and crying, "Oh, I've wrecked our car, I've wrecked our car." She knew what it took to get that car! In the process of turning off the key and lights, I discovered that my back was injured. The horn continued to honked for some time. One of Calvin's hands was pinned under the car. He and I pulled it free, but the process cut and damaged it badly. Royce seemed unhurt but was crying from sheer terror. We carried blankets up the steep embankment and placed them at the side of the road for Calvin and Royce. I waved as a car passed, but it did not stop. They could not possibly see the wrecked car. A second car stopped and took us to Mountainair to the three-cornered house where, by 1940, Uncle Roy lived with his family. They had lost a daughter, Dixie Jo, in Tererro and chose to leave the harsh winters. Suddenly, Mom realized she had left her purse in the wrecked car. When someone brought it, only the money was gone. We phoned Dad. By morning I could not even sit on the indoor chamber from under the bed, without help; there was yet no indoor plumbing in the three-cornered house. Dad borrowed a car in Hot Springs and came to get us. He sold the tires and battery from the wrecked car; that is all they could salvage. Mother Spencer did return with us to Hot Springs for the visit. An osteopath, Dr. Frost, came to our house to give me treatments for my back so I could return to school. He had a daughter, Helen, in my class at school. He told me that when his daughter was born in a hot month in Hot Springs, a line in the local newspaper read, "There Was a Little Frost in Town Last Night." My parents quickly got another car and drove me to school for a short while. That was the start of a lifetime of back problems for me.

I completed my junior year in Hot Springs. Dad quit his job at Carrie Tingley Hospital, and we moved to Arizona. There were parties, socials, and all kinds of good-bye functions. We had lived there four whole years—a record. Our family sold our adobe house, which we had made with our own hands and which held so many good memories. We had built a screened-in porch across the east front of the double garage. Some of us could sleep there if the sparse rain, infrequent snow, or frequently blowing sand permitted. That house has been enlarged by whoever bought it. It is still there in northwest Truth or Consequences, New Mexico, but the hills around are also covered with houses. Look closely; you can see it from Alaska-to-Mexico I-25 as it circles TorC on your way to Las Cruces.

After a day's journey on August 22, 1941, we moved into a very old and dirty house in Clifton, Arizona. As usual, Mom got us all involved, and the house was soon livable. I scrubbed while Calvin and Royce fetched clean water and emptied dirty water. Mae washed windows and put up curtains. Dad found employment at once in Morenci. We shopped in nearby Duncan. Several families were meeting in homes for church. We met the Henderson, O'Day, Heinz, Phillips, and Ollen families and more. Some teenagers were Penny, Chloe, Bertie, Betty, June, and Raymond. In September 1941, my brothers and I enrolled in the Clifton School. In one class, I was assigned to give an oral report on a subject of interest to me. Finally, I got to report on the longest tramway and our trip to the Royal Gorge Bridge, Grand Canyon, Petrified Forest, Oak Creek Canyon, and Sedona. They were impressed, and I scored well on content and presentation. I discovered I could speak if I felt I knew more about my subject than the listeners.

June Henderson and Penny O'Day, friends at church, said they were leaving to attend a private school in Texas. Before they left, they told Mae and me about Southwestern Assemblies of God High School and Business College in Fort Worth. We did not know such a school existed. It cost money to attend; we felt our parents could never afford it. Besides, I had already enrolled in the Clifton Public School and Mae was job-hunting. The task was left to talk with Dad and Mom about the school in Texas. To our surprise, they were interested.

In less than two months from the time we left Hot Springs, Mae and I enrolled at dear ole Southwestern in Fort Worth, Texas. We had never been that far away from home in our lives. There were bells! A bell awoke you, called you to pray, announced meals, rang for chapel and classes, tolled for study hall, and finally rang for lights out. We counted them; there were fifty-seven per day! Someone rang the bell in the middle of the night once. Sheer pandemonium: we thought the place was on fire! Once, the boys hid the bell; the school could not function. P. C. Nelson was president of Southwestern Bible Institute. It was claimed that he was one of five most learned men in America, that he knew more than twenty languages and had more than ten thousand books in his library; some of which he wrote. O. W. Keys was superintendent of both the business college and the high school. Mae enrolled in business college. Evelyn Vaden, Ruth Anderson, and Velma Martin taught in both the high school and the college. I enrolled as a senior in SBI High School. E. W. Moore was principal and senior class sponsor. Other faculty for the high school included Joseph Gutel, Iva Batterton, and Kenzy Savage. (I was familiar with that last name. When he visited the summer camp at Mountainair, New Mexico, he was drafted to sing, "Forty Years Ago," when he was not yet forty!) Mae and I could incorporate classes from the Bible school curriculum into our schedule. That faculty included M. E. Collins and William B. McCafferty. Russell E. Pratt and others taught music.

Annie Bamford was the dorm mother. Rules required us to wear long-sleeved, navy blue uniforms with white, starched cuffs and collars. The distance from skirt hem to floor was measured. Our abode was Dorm Four, up three stairwells (no elevators) to the top floor, and had no walls to divide bed after bed. Mae and I slept together in a double bed. Our dorm mates were, at one time or another, Katherine Herbal, Willie Mae Dunton, Mary Francis Davis, Jane Rouse, Elsie Yates, Margaret Romaine, Aimee Sanlin, Lois Smith, Doris Dyke, Mina Hartsler, Lurlene Fogle, and Janice Meeks. For initiation into Dorm Four, we were to kneel and pray the Siamese Prayer, "Owa Tagu Siam." As we aped the leader faster and faster, the prayer became, "Oh, what a goose I am." Beds were short sheeted or sewed shut. One day, I saw a pair of men's trousers hanging in our one bathroom. Women were not allowed to wear pants at SBI, so I asked why the pants. The owner said she put them there and was praying daily for God to fill them. Mae had her nineieenth birthday within a month after we arrived. She got a cake from home. There was a can of hot tamales *in case they did not eat chili in Texas.* One day when I was sick and alone, I opened the can; it had spoiled and started spraying the ceiling. I was so surprised that I dropped it on the floor; it vented its pressure under the bed. As each student reached a certain level coming up the stairwell, I heard, "Peuu!" The nauseating odor took days to go away. Once I was rudely awakened from a nap by a mouse playing in my hair. It escaped, but a few days later I came into the dorm and there were four newborn pink mice in a nest on top of my bed. The mother fled. I flushed the babies and felt terribly guilty.

On December 7, 1941, Japan bombed Pearl Harbor; the entire school was glued to the radio. Reportedly, three ships were sunk, more than 2,600 American servicemen killed, and more than ten thousand taken captive at different places in the Pacific Arena. The next day, President Roosevelt declared war on Japan and gave his famous, "This day will live in infamy" speech. (My sister, Mae, had no way of knowing it, but her future husband was in Pearl Harbor at that moment!) The Office of Price Administration soon educated us on how to use war ration books for sugar, butter, meat, and other items. The books were given to the school cafeteria where we ate. Mae and I were fortunate that Klaude and Gracie Kendrick drove to Phoenix, Arizona, for Christmas. He was dean of men at SBI and she was the dietician. We rode with them to be with our family in Clifton, Arizona. They went on to Phoenix for the holidays and then picked us up on the return journey. It was a fast trip. The first day back in Fort Worth, it snowed. Some students from South Texas and southern states had never seen snow. They enjoyed the snow; we enjoyed their reactions. The school routine was quickly back to normal. Few students could afford to pay full tuition, so all students had to volunteer some sort of work around the school. Katherine Herbal, Jane Rouse, Lurlene Fogle, and I were assigned to the laundry. We contracted scabies from some of the boy's dirty clothing as they returned from Christmas vacation. Mother Bamford, dean of women, inspected the girls who worked in the laundry when scabies was reported among the boys. We had a few blebs on our hands and were grounded. We could not go to class, meals, or study hall for a few days. Our meals were brought on trays. Dorm Four members kept asking questions because we didn't look sick. We were not allowed out on campus except evenings when all others were in study hall. We took a bath morning and night and applied sulfur and lard to our bodies. The boys' dorm was separate from our dorm, but their shower was in our basement. We itchsisters took shifts sitting at the window to learn which boys came to shower twice a day. We found who had brought the scabies and made sure they knew! One evening, Katherine and I went walking at dusk. We met Clifton Clem, a high school senior from Roswell, New Mexico. He said, "Watch out, or you'll give those cows the itch." We thought the secret was ours; maybe he had scabies! Katherine almost cried. I thought it was funny. While at SBI, the pain in my stomach, which had plagued me since birth, intensified. It may have been because my back still hurt from the wreck. I was prayed for in chapel. One day, Mother Bamford laid her hands on me and prayed with great empathy. I knew that milk and crackers helped reduce the pain in my abdomen temporarily. The cook caught me in the kitchen once trying to find some milk to go with my crackers. Now I was a thief! I spent many nights in the bathtub with a blanket and pillow so I would not groan and wake up others in the dorm. I even studied there! One more thing added to my stress. Mae received a letter from the Civil Service Department. She had passed the test in Las Cruces soon after her high school graduation. Now they were offering her a position with Social Services in Lordsburg, New Mexico. On January

31, 1942, she left Southwestern. Dorm Four girls gave her a farewell party, and we all went to the bus station to see her off. She and I were so close in age, and we had never been so many miles apart before. I missed her terribly.

In Wednesday morning chapel, January 28, 1942, we celebrated the birthday of President P. C. Nelson. Usually, visitors like F. D. Davis, Guy Shields, Raymond Ritchie, or missionaries spoke in chapel. It kept me reminded that, although few people knew it, I expected to go to Africa someday. One day I saw a thin, blond headed boy, about eight years of age, in the school's sweet shop. Someone said, "That is Paul Crouch. His parents are missionaries to Egypt and are visiting churches in Texas." He looked like a small version of what we see on TBN-TV today.

Chapels, usually lead by Kenny Savage, were different. Once, we had a Jericho March around the outside of the school building. The Holy Spirit ministered to young lives in various ways. I saw two students hold a conversation in a language no one understood. Another student said she had taken lessons in an African language. Some students had visions of certain places where they felt God was saying they would someday minister. How presumptive of man, should we try to decide how God can or cannot communicate. The very thought reminds me of the Lois A. Cheney's book, *God Is No Fool* (Cheney 1969). On Sundays, and again Wednesday evenings, we went in groups to different church services. My diary says "Went to Filbert's church," "Went to Braun's church," or "Went to Stewart's church." Some were in Dallas, some in Fort Worth. On the way to church one Sunday, we saw houses and businesses totally under water; the Trinity River had flooded. Southwestern was up on a hill. Churches sometimes provided transportation for students. James Bates often took our group to the church his dad, A. C. Bates, pastored. The three-lane traffic terrified me. Cars, including ours, darted here and there. Hey, neither Hot

Springs, New Mexico, nor Clifton, Arizona, had a *traffic light*. Bates was another name that I associated with New Mexico. A. C. Bates had been the district superintendent of the Texaco District Council of the Assemblies of God in the 30s. That district included New Mexico and West Texas. Part of that time he had no car; he thumbed rides. At New Mexico camp meetings, Reverend Bates often sang a song, which said, "My shoulders are stooped by the weight of years." The teenagers in the congregation often sang along with him, "My shoulders are stooped by the weight of my *ears*." They meant no disrespect; we all loved Brother Bates. My mother, a relatively new Christian in 1939, was a delegate from her local church to a district council in Amarillo, Texas, when the Texaco District was split into two Districts, West Texas and New Mexico. After that decision, H. Milt Fulfer, from Mountainair, was the first district superintendent of our newly formed New Mexico District Council.

At SBI, I took lessons in piano, guitar, and comptometer, the pre-cursor of the calculator. One day, O. W. Keys said, "There is a civil service test available for the comptometer; I would like you to take it." These were opportunities not always available in public schools. My diary sometimes said I made top score in civics or English literature. At mail call, packages or a little money came from my parents or my sister, Mae. Oh, yes, nylon hose were part of the dress code. One day Mae sent nylons. What a lucky girl I was! The school fees were kept as low as possible so that even students such as I could be there. All America was just squeaking out of the vast financial depression. The school itself received donations, items like one hundred pounds of pinto beans or a whole beef, from an individual, church, or district. The cafeteria served a lot of oatmeal for breakfast, pinto beans for lunch, and peanut butter and syrup for supper. Several times, students brought meal trays to me when I was ill. At one point, the tables turned; instead of working in the laundry, my work requirement was to deliver meal trays to ill students.

Mother Bamford was not well. We prayed a lot for her, as she did for us. On Sunday, April 12, 1942, I had not gone to church, as I was not feeling well. At 9:50 A.M., Mother Bamford died. She was a lady! It was reported that her last words were, "Jesus, this is Annie Bamford." It was a subdued dorm for many days. Madilyn Ballard (Bracket eventually) had been Mother Bamford's right-hand helper. She and Catherine McCafferty completed that year as housemothers for the women.

On May 3, 1942, I was eighteen. My birthday was eclipsed by final exams and multiple activities around high school graduation. Our senior class trip was to Justin Boot Factory, the airport at Love Field, Texas Wesleyan College, Botanic Gardens, Baird's Bakery, and Light Crust Flour Mill with music by the Dough Boys.

Cards came with money or other gifts. They came from Mom, Dad, and two brothers. They arrived from Aunt Della Carpenter in Colorado, Mom Wallace, and Annelle in Amarillo. A Western Union Telegram came from my sister, Mae, while Aunt Olivia sent a watch from San Francisco. Life was looking up! Things were happening so fast. Graduation practice: our chapel was too small for all the visitors from Texas and other states, so all exercises took place in North Fort Worth High School. My parents did not come; I did not expect them. They did well to send me to school. On May 28, our hopes and egos were boosted at the baccalaureate service. At the commencement exercises on May 29, we received that long-waited high school diploma, signed by President P. C. Nelson, Superintendent O. W. Keys, Principal E. W. Moore, District Superintendent F. D. Davis, District Secretary C. P. Robison, and Ellis County Superintendent of Schools A. D. Roach. Clary Anthony was our senior class student president, and Dorothy Lee Green was our class valedictorian. I received honors in civics and a medal for English literature. The statement under my name in our yearbook, said, "Quietness is beauty in its best estate." Hey, "Quietness can also result in ulcers. Jude 2."

# CHAPTER 6

# San Francisco, WWII
# Phoenix, Teletype

NOTHER WORLD IN MY life began. It is shocking to be propelled back into to the *unreal world* after experiencing Southwestern. I pondered on what to do. I was not a student any longer. I could go to my parents' home in Arizona, but I had lived there less than two months before going to SBI. In my heart, New Mexico was still home. I was determined not to depend on Dad and Mom for long. On Saturday, May 30, Sterling Elms, June Henderson, Penny O'Day, Raymond Hatler, and I left the big Dallas-Fort Worth area in the dark and headed back to the wild, wild, West in a trusty ole vehicle belonging to Sterling. Tires and gasoline were rationed. America was at war. After traveling all night, we stopped just long enough for breakfast with Sterling's aunt in Odessa.

When we set out on our journey again, a tire blew almost immediately. We put on the spare; two hours later it blew. The sun was extremely hot. Four of us sat in the shade of a signboard while Sterling hitched a ride and brought back a used tire. An hour later, it went flat. Then we waited in a downpour of rain until a car stopped. Their rims fit our wheels. The driver believed our story about students going home, so he helped put his spare on our car. He followed us into Pecos, Texas, where he retrieved his tire and left. We had no ration coupons for tires; our parents had those. By the time the flat was repaired and we shopped for a used spare, the Pecos River had flooded and we were stranded. I kept a copy of a letter I wrote that night:

> Dear K. J., We just rented a motel room, one room for all five. We three girls grabbed the bed. The springs were coils so we could not even offer the mattress to the boys, who slept on the floor; we did sacrifice the pillows. Oh, if only we had refused those second helpings of beans, peanut butter, and syrup in the school cafeteria. The bed was sturdy, and we slept well.

Next morning we arose to sunshine—and a *flat tire*. We had it repaired and were off again. After one more flat and some sleeping in the car, we got to El Paso, Texas, and on to Lordsburg, New Mexico. The comradery had been pleasant, but the last umbilical cord to SBI was severed at 6:00 A.M. when they left me with my sister, Louella Mae, in Lordsburg. She and I had gone to SBI less than a year ago, so she knew some of the travelers. Most of them were going to Clifton, Arizona; Sterling was from Phoenix.

Mae and I had a lot to talk about, so we went out to eat breakfast. She surprised me with an Agfa Sure Shot camera for my birthday and graduation. It still works after fifty years. After a good night's rest, Mae and I boarded a Greyhound bus to cross just into Arizona. June 4 was Dad's forty-first birthday. We celebrated with cake and ice cream. Calvin still got the ice cream paddle. My parents drove us back to Lordsburg to attend a New Mexico State Youth Convention in Silver City. It seemed strange, as we usually went west from Hot Springs to Silver City for conventions. Friends from all over New Mexico would be there. Ann Pennington, from Silver City, had also gone to SBI in Fort Worth, so she qualified as kin. The youth convention was the success we anticipated. On the way back to Arizona, we dropped Mae off at Lordsburg. We also had a flat tire; one never escaped reminders of the war. As we rode along, Dad remarked, "Everyone is going out to the shipyards in San Francisco. Why don't we go?" Mom said, "Dad, you are a good machinist. With your experience in making parts for your dad's sawmills and the years of providing electricity at Carrie Tingley Hospital, you could be just what they need to repair ships damaged in the war." At home in Arizona, we started planning, having yard sales, throwing away, and packing. On July 7, I was sanding an old sewing machine cabinet to be varnished and sold when a splinter went under my right index fingernail. It extended far up beyond the nail bed, into the finger! We went for medical help. When a doctor prepared to inject a local anesthesia and extract the splinter, I refused due to my irrational fear of needles. Before I became a nurse, I would practically faint at a drop of blood or a needle—anything sharp. I never thought about the anesthesia inside the needle or how it would reduce the pain. The doctor did give me an anti-tetanus injection. When I went home, I managed to get hold of the sticker by scraping through the full length of the nail with a razor blade. I pulled it out, but was never sure I got it all.

We posted notices at the post office and any place that allowed: "A SALE at Bunker Hill Monday, July 20." It worked. On July 22 we went west, leaving Mae far behind in Lordsburg. We left our dog, Tooch, with someone, and we all cried. That day we drove to Safford and all *five* slept in a one-room motel cabin. Deja vu! Been there, done that just a few days before! Alas, my jaws were feeling a bit tight. In Phoenix the next day, we missed Aunt Leonora. She had gone to San Francisco to visit her mom and two sisters. We got a tire vulcanized for the journey, shopped for clothing, and got Mom's first glasses. When a Greyhound bus passed us, Mom exclaimed, "Hey, in New Mexico their buses are gray; here in Arizona, they are blue!" At thirty-seven, she was seeing things for the first time. All her life she had needed glasses as badly as I, but no one knew it. We drove through the hot Arizona desert at night. On Mom's birthday, we were still traveling, but we found ice cream. California was very beautiful. Grass, geraniums, and vines grew on every fence and hillside. We started taking pictures of everything we saw. It was actually night when we finally did see the beautiful, but awesome, Pacific Ocean. We turned north toward San Francisco. When we parked to sleep a bit, we were driven off of private property and knew immediately we were not in the open roads of New Mexico. Dad sang a song, "I saw a little box all painted red, put my letter in it. Whoopee! Gee, what they did to me, squirted water all over me! Dumb ol' root from a high grass town." When our travel money got low in a small town, we stopped a pedestrian and asked for directions to the Employment Agency. She said she did not speak English, so Dad spoke Spanish. She said she knew the way and got into our car. After several miles and many directives, she got out of the car and said in English, "Thank you. This is where I live." Dad sang his song again: "Whoopee! Gee—" We found the agency and got work for the whole family hoeing beans on a farm. Our employer provided a cute little house with cookstove, running water, and a shower. We cleaned house, bathed, and organized for the night. That evening, we dug my guitar from the trailer and the family sang and had devotions. Before sleeping, I wrote to K.J.; I had much to tell. After the first eight hours, we had sore muscles and fever from sunburn, but we worked for five days before we drove to San Francisco on August 5. Our Mamaw Layman lived on Kearney Street, Aunt Charlcie on Turk, and Aunt Olivia on another street. We found an apartment on Fillmore Street. San Francisco was crowded with servicemen's families and people getting jobs to help win the war; people lived wherever necessary. Dad was employed at once; his qualifications were in demand, as we had suspected. He looked at a ship part and made it. Ships were repaired and sent back to battle.

I was only eighteen, so my young Aunt Olivia helped me buy a purse and a saucy hat with a feather on it and went job hunting with me. We located an interesting possibility. San Francisco would have been more shocking to me had I not gone to school in Fort Worth. Postal Telegraph was training teletype operators. On August 10, just five days after my arrival in San Francisco, I signed on for training. You worked from the school right into a job when you were ready. My jaws were gradually loosening, but they often clamped down and cut my tongue.

The first day at work, Dorothy, an operator, asked me where I was from. I said, "New Mexico."

She said, "You don't look like a Mexican."

I said, "Oh, not Mexico, *New* Mexico is a State in the USA."

"Really? I was born in San Francisco and never been outside the city limits."

Then I wondered, "Has she not sent telegrams to New Mexico?" One day, I took some piñons to munch on. Dorothy said, "Oh, pinettes!" "What?" I asked. She said, "Those are pinettes." My mind raced back to New Mexico's mountains where we gathered pinions. I said, "No, they are piñons." She said, "They grow on pine trees." Again, I saw myself making strands of pine-needle beads. You couldn't do that with short piñon needles. I said, "No, they grow on piñon trees." We each learned something and became quite good friends. After eleven days I got a paycheck for $7; it quickly increased to $19.36 per week. My first real job, *ever*! I could start paying my way in life. I was assigned to the evening shift, 4:00 P.M. to midnight. From my workplace at midnight I took the K Car to a corner of Fillmore Street and walked to our building. Mom and Dad trusted that God would take care of me; if I ever had a daughter I would be far too protective. Our apartment was upstairs. Our landlord gave me a key to the entrance door downstairs. One night, I came home from work at midnight, and the key did not fit. I was locked out! A sailor walking by asked if he could help. I backed up and let him try the key. After a serious try, he looked at me and asked, "Are you sure you live here?" I said, "Yes," and quickly added, "with my parents." He walked with me to a corner Tobacco Shop. I must say, I felt safer this way than alone! I phoned the landlord. He came and let me in. I said, "Thank you," to him and the sailor and went upstairs. The landlord had changed the lock for good reason—we were not in a good area of San Francisco. The city was swamped by people coming for shipyard jobs. People had money for drinking and prostitution, but in the hallways and on the stairways, they slept and paid nothing. The landlord gave me a new key after changing the lock. I tried it before I left for work the next day. We started actively hunting a home in a better environment.

I worked in the night, so Mom and I could go shopping in the daytime. We bought the popular Remember Pearl Harbor pin and some hose to send to Mae in Lordsburg. Mom always seemed compelled to give. Weekends found the whole family in Golden Gate Park, or some other beautiful or interesting place, where we took pictures. Glad Tidings Temple was our home church; Reverend Leland Keys was the pastor. The church was a part of Glad Tidings Bible Institute, just around the corner from where we lived. I could take piano lessons and even practice there. One music teacher named Russell Pratt had taught at SBI in Texas. Familiar faces shrunk my world; he had a picture of SBI on his desk. Once there was a reunion of former Southwestern students with picture taking at Glad Tidings Bible Institute.

Normally, when we left church on our way home, we walked up a street, crossed Fillmore, stepped upon a curb and turned left to walk up the sidewalk to our building. One Sunday after attending church, a dream jolted me back into my plans involving Africa. In my dream I walked that same way, except that as I stepped upon the sidewalk at Fillmore Street, there was a triangle sign. It was like a sandwich sign, advertising shoeshines on one side and hamburgers on the other side. This time, there was a map on one side. There was a definite feeling that God had put it there. I looked closely and asked, "And where is that, God?" I stooped to look, and not only did I recognize the map of Africa, but it had the abbreviated word "Afr" inside a square on the west side of the African continent. I awoke saying the words aloud, "No, Lord," over and over. When I was fully awake, I asked, "Why was I saying that? I would never refuse to do what God asked me to do. I was willing in high school, in SBI, and I'm willing now. I will go where God sends me!" However, it never entered my mind to go to Glad Tidings Bible College right at my own home church. Well, I had no money; I could not ask my parents to pay for school again.

My sister, Mae, quit her job in New Mexico and transferred to San Francisco in September 1942. She arrived in time for her own birthday on October 21. It was that big one; she was twenty! We had sold the ice cream freezer in Arizona, but we had cake and ice cream, anyway. Every spare moment, Mom, Mae, and I were house hunting. Dad worked days. Mom was taking correspondence courses. With no formal education, she had gotten a taste of learning, and there was no stopping her. Mae or I typed her lessons before she mailed them to Springfield, Missouri. One day, we found the ideal flat for a family of six; it was on Hyde Street and there were no stairs. Our landlord on Fillmore was not unhappy when we told him we were moving, as our family kept growing. After Mae arrived, I stayed with my Mamaw Layman part time. When the 1453 Hyde Street flat was ready, we painted tables and chairs, bought extra furniture from Sterling and Gray Home Furnishing Company and moved in, all under one roof. Mae and I had a room together again. Dad, Mae, and I had good jobs. Calvin had a paper route, worked in a grocery store, and went to school. Royce sold papers on the street and went to school. Mom did well to cook for six and study. However, we weren't as near to our church, and I commuted to work by a different route. It was still after midnight every night when I rode the little trolley car that rattled and groaned up the hills through Chinatown toward Knob Hill. At Hyde Street, I got off and walked toward the Mark Hopkins Hotel. It was a different neighborhood.

Christmas was creeping up fast. We had more money than we had ever had before, a better house, and a basement large enough to skate in. We shopped for gifts, and wrapped and hid them. On Christmas Eve at my work site, many were celebrating with alcohol and were loud. There were horns, bells, and bottles in our office and on the streets twelve stories below. We could hear the people talking loudly, and two cars collided. I wondered if people even knew that Jesus was the One being celebrated? Some even used His name in vain. At midnight, the little trolley rattled and groaned its way through Chinatown as usual. I got off at Hyde Street and walked up the hill through little groups celebrating in their own way, but I never felt in danger. My family was waiting. We opened our gifts. Mom had not made our gifts from cigar boxes as in years before. In San Francisco, she and Dad bought our last dolls. Mae and I asked for them, as all our dolls had burned in the house fire or been discarded or sold every time we moved. Now we planned to keep the new ones, and we have. We got to bed about 4:00 A.M. on Christmas morning and were up again by noon. Mom had cooked a turkey with a meal only she could prepare. Aunt Charlcie, Aunt Olivia, their husbands, and Mamaw came to help us eat it. I went to work at 4:00 P.M. on Christmas day and worked until midnight. On December 31, I teletyped the old year out and 1943 in.

My back still hurt from the wreck in Mountainair. My jaws locked sporadically. Sometimes my tongue got caught between my teeth when the jaws slammed shut. The jaws would not relax until the tongue slid free; I do not know why. It was slashed and bled profusely as it slid free. My stomach was still gnawing away at itself the same as it had at Southwestern and for most of my life. Mom went with me to the much-advertised Shane's Diagnostic Clinic; I could pay now. The doctor recommended some treatments and put me on a diet of cooked cereal and puréed baby food. Mom, Dad, or both went with me for treatments weekly for a month. Work, piano lessons, cable car rides, church, and Golden Gate Park made life diverse and interesting. These activities were handsful wedged on purpose between sirens at midnight for war blackouts, earth tremors that swung our chandeliers, and bad news of servicemen killed in the war. Due to rationing points for such items as sugar, butter, meat, honey, Postum, shoes, and hose, shopping became quite a chore. Black pepper was scarce; we hated the white pepper.

On February 2, I went job hunting and took a civil service exam for teletye operator. Mae had a civil service job and was making more money than I ever would at Postal Telegraph. I found there was a civil service position available in Phoenix. What, back to Arizona? Well, Aunt Leonora lived in Phoenix with her husband, Nevin, and my cousins, Lester, Robert, and Catherine. Lester was not at home. He was a U.S. pilot in the European Theater. He and my sister, Mae, had been born in Mountainair's three-cornered house the same week, so he had just turned twenty, yet his crew in Italy called him "the old man." I really felt good about going back to Arizona. The man who interviewed me quoted possible civil service ratings and salaries. To live alone, I would need enough money to be my sole provider. I reported my decision to the interviewer, "If I can begin at the highest salary that you quoted, I will accept the assignment." His reply was, "You are very fortunate, at your age, to demand such wages." He was right; I was still only eighteen. The Postal Telegraph Company merged with Western Union soon after I resigned in San Francisco, so Postal Telegraph is no more.

On Saturday, March 27, Mom and I went shopping. I bought some clothing and a Bible. At 8:00 P.M., I boarded a bus to Los Angeles. Not surprisingly, my seat partner was a serviceman; they were everywhere, thank God! Mom Wallace and Annelle (Mabel's mom and sister) had moved from Amarillo, Texas, to work in Wilmington. They met my bus. That evening, they took me to Amie Simple McPherson's Angeles Temple to see the story of salvation in drama. Elsie, Mom Wallace's older daughter, and her husband, Shorty Carl, had moved from the Ruidoso-Carrizozo area in New Mexico to Van Nuys. Shorty was driving for mass transit in the greater L.A. area. I visited them all on my way to my new job. Then I rushed off to Arizona, where Aunt Leonora met me at the Greyhound bus Depot in Phoenix. I was genuinely excited to be there.

On March 31, 1943, the day after my arrival, I started teletyping for OWI-CAS, (Office of War Information-Central Administrative Services). We were seven floors up in the Security Building on Central Avenue in Phoenix. Some of my teletype sisters were Thelma, Tillie, Esther, Norma, and Millie. Mr. Joseph Cardani was our boss. His assignment was to supply furniture, equipment, typewriters, and office supplies to OPA and other government agencies. We sent classified telegrams, orders, and letters for war agencies. We also received and sent telegrams for Japanese Americans in relocation camps. We sent telegrams to help them run their businesses while they were absent from them. We received as many as 495 TWXs from Casa Grande at one time to send for Japanese Americans.

I stayed with Aunt Leonora the first month in Phoenix, and then I went on my own. For a while, I moved in with Mae Livengood and her mother. That was another Mae in my life other than my sister. I made friends with her whole family for a lifetime. (Eventually, Mae married and had two sons and a daughter. As a nurse-midwife, I have specialized in other people's babies. My fridge is plastered with pictures of other people's children from more than one continent. I call them my grandkids and they are special.)

Friends at the Phoenix First Assembly were many: Cleo, Marjorie (she became a WWII nurse), Juanita, Nadine, Faith, Elma Lou, Grant, Earl, Charles, Jennie, Anna Mae, Alice, and Mae. (Alice went to SAGU in Waxahachie when I did. She married Ron Hazard, and they raised a delightful family of four in Wisconsin. They supported me the whole time I was in Africa.) Mae (Livengood) Cohea remained a good friend and kept me informed through the years about her family and my many friends in the Phoenix church. From the Livengood home, I moved across town to West Polk into a garret housekeeping room. I had always been with people and did not know how important an alarm clock was. The first Sunday alone in my lean-to, I asked God to awaken me in time for church. At the right time, I fell out of bed for the first and only time in my life. *I bought a clock!* I had my nineteenth birthday while working in Phoenix; my family phoned from San Francisco to my job site. Secular work, still a six-day workweek, drained me. One teletype operator used such language that I finally suggested that if she must vent, to please leave God, my Best Friend, out of it. She really tried to follow my suggestion. My work and looking forward to Sunday at First Assembly at Eleventh and Garfield became my life. I loved having tithes (and even income tax) to pay. Sundays were for my spiritual refueling. Rev. N. D. Davidson, his wife, and six sons were my pastors. Their oldest son, Rex, was killed in the European theater. That family so impressed me that I vowed to have a ball team of sons someday.

Phoenix experienced a devastating flood while I was there. Aunt Leonora's adobe home was badly damaged. She told me that she took refuge on a haystack out in the middle of a field and was ever so surprised at the useless items she had salvaged when she grabbed things in such a hurry. Luckily, the haystack did not float away. Mrs. Ridell, a friend, and I went out for two days to help dig out mud. I believe the ruined books depressed me most. The lean-to (garret) I rented was dark and became too small. I moved to a larger, well-lighted bedroom with kitchen privileges on Taylor Street. My new address was near a streetcar and more convenient to my work and church.

My sister, Mae, worked with the War Manpower Commission in San Francisco where they not only helped people to be in the job where they wanted to be, but to be where they were needed most for the war effort. She located the OWI-CAS office in San Francisco and asked them to contact the operators in our Phoenix OWI-CAS office. She wanted to know the dates of my vacation so she could get off at that same time and we could visit my parents, who had moved to the Napa Valley, northeast of San Francisco. At my job, we talked with our fingers on a keyboard onto a visual screen. It cut holes into paper tape that would save the message and could be used to print the message again. That sounds like my present computer, except that is used tape for saving rather than a disc. After only six months with OWI-CAS, I took two weeks off to go see Dad and Mom. The train was hot and crowded. We had to stand in hallways or sit on our own luggage; it seemed like the longest night of my life. Next morning, the conductor announced, "San Francisco!" Mae and my Aunt Olivia Irene were there to meet me. We went to the SF-OWI-CAS office so I could notify my fellow Phoenix workers of my safe arrival. Names and code numbers in the San Francisco offices became faces of real people. I had been teletyping to them for six months. Someone gave me a very descriptive "Dirge Of A Teletype Operator":

> *There are many jobs in this world to be had.*
> *Some of them good; some of them bad,*
> *But brother, we gals with the bruises and blisters,*
> *Belong to the order of "Teletype Sisters."*
> *When the sun descends in a rosy glow,*
> *And others are free to come and go,*

*With a masculine arm on which to lean*
*We sit up here nursing a noisy machine.*

*Then again, when the world is asleep in bed,*
*And we fain would rest our weary head,*
*Our alarm goes off and it's four-fifteen,*
*And we stagger down town to that waiting machine.*

*Oh, the hours are crazy, the joys are few,*
*But here is a secret, I'll tell it to you,*
*Our life's never dull and in spite of the blisters,*
*We really enjoy being Teletype Sisters.*

—BAC

Then Mae and I went apartment hunting for her and found one. We went to Chinatown and bought house slippers for my Phoenix Teletype sisters. Dad, Mom, Calvin, and Royce drove to San Francisco and took me to Napa. They had a nice car and a trailer house, but they were *picking prunes*. Dad, always the teacher, was very excited to teach me the processing of prunes from tree to packaging, and it was interesting. If you weren't a good learner, he would use a screwdriver or any tool handy to plunk you on the knuckles or head. He had taught me the multiplication tables, how to make adobe bricks, drive a car, shoot a gun, hunt rabbits and deer, repair a car with bailing wire—*and now prunes! I did pick!* Napa was far enough from the ocean to escape the heavy dampness but close enough to let the fog roll in over the hills at evening time and out in the morning as the sun warmed the air. What a beautiful place to live. Mae came from San Francisco for the weekend before I left Saturday evening. All six of us were together in Napa. We had our very last family group picture taken. Mom made sure these family things happened. On my way back to Phoenix, I stopped near Los Angeles for a visit with my Uncle Johnny Layman and Aunt Lois (Garret). Again, I went to the L.A. offices of OWI-CAS. They notified the Phoenix office that I was on my way back. Then at the last minute, I was bumped from the train's passenger list to make room for a sailor. When they did get me on the train, my seatmate was an Air Force lieutenant. We talked about our shrinking world and about our grandparents, who came west by wagon train and saw the world as an opportunity for growth without end. The train delivered me swiftly and safely to Phoenix. My co-workers liked their Chinatown slippers and even bought the pair I got for myself.

Calvin, my brother, was traveling close behind me. He visited with Aunt Leonora's family and me in Phoenix. He had worked and saved money in California on paper routes and in grocery stores, and he was on his way to high school at SBI. He was sixteen, a sophomore.

Southwestern Bible Institute had moved from Fort Worth, where I had attended, into much better facilities in Waxahachie, Texas. To stretch his funds, Calvin worked with the school maintenance man, Mr. Gordon. Near Thanksgiving in 1943, Royce had his eleventh birthday. I mailed him defense stamps. I spent the holiday season with Aunt Leonora and her family in north Phoenix. I felt comfortable living and working in Phoenix; my health improved. When my Taylor Street landlord started singing, "Love Lifted Me," while his wife was at work, I moved again, to an apartment on East Van Buren Street. On my twentieth birthday, I went to the ladies lounge at work and cried; I would never be a teenager again. Those were the years when I had collected positive memories. Within a few years, I had come a long way from the tents in the mountains and the adobe farmhouse with a dirt floor to a livable paycheck of my own.

Again, I was jolted by a dream. In the dream, a group was at a home prayer meeting. We were on our knees. An audible voice, similar to prophesy, spoke. At the time I felt it was the Lord reminding me again of Africa. The Voice said,

"Get up and go to Bible College; *I have something I want you to do*." This triggered my memory about a sequence of events:

- Mabel and I had talked, by the time we were 14, about going somewhere as missionaries. (In the 1990s Annelle, Mabel's sister, sent me a copy of a play I helped Mabel write about missions for our youth group. See Appendix.) I had a dream about feeding sheep from a basket just before Mabel died.

- Homer and Thelma Goodwin, the first missionaries I ever heard, made an impression. However, I did not know where their field, the Gold Coast, was.

- In Southwestern High School, I continued to feel the call. It was always to Africa, maybe an orphanage in Egypt.

- The dream in San Francisco, with the map of Africa with the little notation, Afr, nudged me like, "Hey, I'm reminding you."

In a mission service, at Eleventh and Garfield First Assembly in Phoenix, I made the final decision. I would go to Southwestern and major in Bible and missions. I talked with my pastor. He said, "You have such a good job. You are so shy in youth services or when you speak in church." I said, "True. I do not understand it, either, but it seems the Lord will not let me forget. So I will go to Southwestern and see what God has planned."

When I told my boss, Mr. Cardani, that I was resigning, he said, "Well, if it is overseas appointment you want, I can get you located. Where do you want to go?" He cupped his hands together, holding them up high as if he were holding liquid in them. He said, "Pennies from heaven; name your place and price." I tried to explain that it was not for money, but for a definite call I felt to present the Gospel to people who did not know Jesus as their Hope. When I said that I would go under the mission board of my church, he said,

"But you could go anywhere you wanted and get paid. A mission will pay very little." "True," I said.

I left my Van Buren apartment and went to Southwestern. My last day as teletype operator at OWI-CAS in Phoenix was September 30, 1944. I had worked there for eighteen months. My co-workers bade me farewell with a party. The time was right to actively obey God's call. I put on my blinders; I set my goals. Nothing could hinder me from doing whatever it was God wanted me to do. I would:

- **Feed my faith in Christ,** God's Son, so I would have a message for Africa. I read somewhere, "Feed your faith and your doubts will starve to death." Or, don't let just anyone brainwash you; decide for yourself what you want in your brain.

- **Actively pursue the requirements** to fulfill the call that I had felt for so long.

- **Say very little** about my plan; *just do.* If God wanted me there, He would get me there; if not, no one would require an explanation.

On Sunday, October 1, 1944, in First Assembly at Eleventh and Garfield Streets, I was asked to come forward and say good-bye in the Sunday school class, morning worship service, and again in the evening youth service. I left by bus at 2:45 P.M. on Monday to return to SBI. Esther Deason, a girl just out of high school and also from First Assembly, was going to SBI, and we rode together. She was a new Christian and waiting for her special man to return from the service. She told me all about him three times a day! We traveled all day Tuesday and arrived in Waxahachie, Texas, on Wednesday, October 4. My brother, Calvin, was still at SBI. He was beginning his junior year in high school. We were very glad to see each other. He and I traveled to Dallas the first Saturday after I arrived. I wanted to visit the Dallas OWI-CAS office and replace code numbers with faces and names as I had in Los Angeles. I thought that there might be an opening for part-time work, maybe weekends. There was not. A few days after this trip, Calvin, whom I still called Sonny, became very ill with appendicitis. It was frightening as we were so far from our parents. Many at the school were praying for him, and he improved in a few days.

Because I was a more mature student, I was given a room in the basement level of the girl's dorm. Rae Elliott was also older, so she was given a room next to mine. I had never met her, although she was from a church in Phoenix. Esther Deason was allowed to room with me. She stayed only a very short time and went to California to marry her U.S. serviceman, Leon Felton. The prayer room, where I spent a lot of time, was also conveniently located in the basement.

1. Sisters, Charlese and Mae. 2. Mamaw Lula Layman and me. Employed at Postal Telegraph, San Francisco. 3. Phoenix Teletype Operator. 4. Teletype sisters. Top: Thelma Bay, Phoenix supervisor. Lower: Geneva Jones, San Francisco supervisor. Standing: Charlese. Seven stories up looking north, up Central Avenue toward Hilton Hotel in Phoenix. 5. Group of ministers at Assemblies of God camp in Arizona. 6. Esther Deason went to SBI for a short time with me. 7. Our last family portrait.

1. Pastor N.D. Davidson family, of First Assembly, 11th and Garfield, in Phoenix. 2-4. First Assembly friends: Nadine Kimbro, Jenny Powell, Cleo Eastman, Marjorie Sherrick, Mae Livengood, me, and Alice Wall. 5-5a. Aunt Leonora, cousins Lester, Robert, and Kathy, and my brother, Calvin Lee via PX 1944 to SBI HS. 6-9 My SBI friends: Thelma R-W, Louise D, Ester D-F, "Going our way," B&CM Caferty, FEA. with Calvin. In memory of: Grace D-E-S and her niece, Norma Jean T-B (with me #7).

CHAPTER 7

# *Waxahachie and Albuquerque Blinders*

ON ENROLLMENT DAY AT Southwestern, I found that I could transfer Bible credits, completed there in high school, toward bible school requirements. That would allow me to graduate in two years, as opposed to three, if I enrolled in a heavy load of classes, or a summer session. I could also challenge courses such as English. The money I had saved in Phoenix disappeared quickly on fees and books. I had no source of income, so I cleaned houses and helped a very ill lady in the town. Within a few days, I got a job in the Southwestern Book Store, Post Office, and Sweet Shop. Grace Davis was the manager. We got very busy as servicemen returned from the war and chose Southwestern for their education under the GI Bill. We ordered and sold textbooks and reference books. We sold Bibles, stamps, candy, and other snacks. With this mixture, mice were a problem; while looking for food, they chewed on the books. We got a cat and named him Lance after the company that delivered snacks for the students. I was constantly teased that the cat's coat was the same color as my red-blond hair. Grace, the students, and I became fond of Lance. He didn't need to hunt mice among the books for food. Grace even bought him raw liver. We thought she was being good to him, but after some time, he got worms and died. Lance was buried on campus and mourned by many.

Sometimes, I still did not have money for a three-cent stamp to write home. My earnings were applied to my tuition. Once, Louise Driskill handed me an envelope and would not tell me who sent it. It contained five dollars. Such as this was quite common in the lives of Southwestern students who needed help to remain in school. Then, someone phoned from the local Western Union to ask if I needed work on weekends and at nights, so I became relief operator, but it shortened my study time. My brother, Calvin, left Southwestern because of financial problems. He went to our parents, who had returned from California and were pastoring a church and farming in Corona, New Mexico. Rae Elliott also left school, as the courts awarded her custody of her two daughters. Dean Hargis did not want me in the basement level alone. She ordered me to move upstairs. Each room had two or more bunk beds that allowed four or more students per room. Some of my roommates were Shirley Jones, Mary Gray, Ethel McClendon, and Thelma Roark. I made lifelong friends. While other students were sleeping, I would study by flashlight in a clothes closet. I did not have money to go home for Christmas 1944, but when school was out in June 1945, I went to Mountainair, New Mexico, where Mom and Dad had bought a Help-'Ur-Self laundry. The State Camp Ground of the Assemblies of God was located there. During youth camps, there were not enough dorm rooms on the campground, so some campers stayed at our house. There were sleeping bags in the laundry and the garage, and in our house. Gloria Gray McLaughlin and others I met in later years said how grateful they were to my parents. During family camp times, I ironed white shirts for hours for preachers. I taught a class in Sunday school at the local Assembly. I also painted the walls of my parents' front room, where I was sleeping on their divan. One day, my parents and I drove to Albuquerque, where they bought me the piano that I still own. My Mamaw Layman kept it for me while I was in schools and in Africa.

In late summer of 1945, Mary Gray, one of my roommates at SBI, had scheduled two revivals in New Mexico. She was a native New Mexican, as I was. She invited me to come and help. One Monday, I took the train to Albuquerque. Mary and Pauline met me at the depot. Pauline (McQeary) Jernigan, Opal Mae (Toothman) Wells, and Reta (Hotchkiss) Hall had conducted revivals around New Mexico before they were married. Mary and I stayed at the home of Mark and Pauline Jernigan during that revival effort. Jane and Eddie Mae, two of our SBI friends who worked at the capitol in Santa Fe, came down to visit us for the weekend. The four of us piled onto one bed because we had so much to talk about and we did not want to disturb the host family. The slats collapsed and we fell to the floor in a thunderous roar! Mark teased us for years about breaking down their bed and waking them. We were guilty!

Reverend and Mrs. Watkins were the pastors of Five Points Assembly in South Albuquerque. Mary preached and played the accordion and the piano; I played the guitar. We both sang. After the successful meeting, Mary's mom and two sisters, Freeda and Teresa, drove us to Belen, where they lived at the time. I rode a train on to Mountainair where I packed my belongings for a final year at SBI. My two brothers, Calvin and Royce, drove me to Willard, where I got on the same Greyhound bus that Mary Gray had boarded in Albuquerque. The second meeting Mary had scheduled was with Reverend and Mrs. Vowell at Lovington Assembly in southern New Mexico on our way back to SBI in Texas. Mary preached, and we had children's church and street meetings. I cut and sewed a uniform for school. We were still wearing navy dresses, but with not-so-stiff collars.

As a farewell, the church showered us with stationery,

hose, and powder. A Greyhound bus delivered us to SBI in Waxahachie at 6:00 P.M. on October 1. The very next day, we enrolled for another semester, and I went back to work in the bookstore. On October 15, my diary says, "I got five dollars from Mom." I put a sign on my dorm door: "Perms, pin curls, and waves. Bring your own pins and clamps."

Reverend and Mrs. Murray Brown, missionaries to West Africa, came to Southwestern and spoke in morning chapel. In the afternoon, he spoke to a group of boys and she spoke to the girls. She told us, "Mission work is changing; countries are interested in what we have to offer their people. They are not concerned, as we are, with giving out the Good News of Jesus." The question was asked, "What can single women contribute?" She replied, "Teachers and nurses are needed." I knew I would never have enough money to go to teacher's college. As I often say, "My head was made up!" I would train to be a nurse. I did wonder what I would do about fainting at the sight of a drop of blood or something sharp like a knife or needle.

The immediate reality consisted of classes and work. On Sundays, students were assigned to go to churches in towns near or within a triangle formed by Waxahachie, Dallas, and Fort Worth. This was like clinical practice, but they called it outstation work. We went in groups to Midlothian, Ennis, Milford or Red Oak. (Some say my Grandfather Layman's siblings were born at Red Oak. That was not far from where I graduated twice, from high school in Fort Worth and from bible college in Waxahachie.)

Our Dean Hargis resigned. We girls from Arizona gave her a meal and a sweater for a going-away gift. The school presented her with a suitcase and money. A girl named Ollie filled the interim until Dorm Dean Campbell arrived. My stomach did not do well on school-cafeteria fare. My back hurt from lifting books and sitting long in classes. My jaws still locked occasionally. It was not easy to balance being a student and managing my health; I had done better in the basement. While checking rooms, Ollie found me in bed one Monday when I was not feeling well and was exercising some of my maturity and independence. I should have been somewhere on schedule; I soon was.

A letter came from my sister Mae who still lived and worked in San Francisco. She wrote, "Dave's ship is leaving Japan on October 22 to return to the States." On November 21, 1945, my only sister, Louella Mae, and David E. Lynch were married by Rev. Leland Keys at Glad Tidings Temple in San Francisco. Because of a war emergency, Dave was called back to his ship, and it sailed the day after they married. I had no money to travel from Texas to California for a wedding. (Mae and Dave celebrated their fiftieth wedding anniversary in November 1995; I went to that!) I even stayed at school for Christmas the holiday season of 1945, as I had no money to travel. The school held the accustomed New Year's watch night service on the last night of December. As we were gathering to start, someone from behind slammed a hat on top of my head so hard that it almost covered my eyes. I wondered who knew me that well. I turned, and it was my dad. What a surprise! He and my mom were on a trip to Arkansas. This was their first visit to Southwestern in all the years Mae, Calvin, or I had been there. They left on New Year's Day, 1946.

Just as the students were returning from holidays, a freezing rain hit the area; ice hung from every tree. It was beautiful, but I had never seen this in New Mexico or Arizona. During that ice storm we enrolled for the spring semester. I took a journalism test and passed it so I could skip English IV. All corners were cut so I could graduate sooner. Classes started; there were assignments to complete. I still worked at Western Union, on occasion, and in the bookstore. I was often asked to show visitors through the school. At the end of a very busy year, there were school weddings, parties, and tearful farewells in several places within the town of Waxahachie. As we walked back from a party in the town, a very sincere young gentleman walked back with me and begged me to marry him. I put on my blinders again. Since romance is not an objective of this book, all gentlemen who have shown an interest in me shall remain safely and respectfully nameless.

On May 24, 1946, I graduated without a diploma; my transcript lacked a few credits. To receive my diploma would not require a full semester of work. I planned to leave school, work, and save money to return for the 1947 summer session. In the meantime, I went back to my parents' home in Mountainair, New Mexico. They had sold their laundry and were living on the north side of town.

Mom, Dad, and my two brothers had remodeled the house. There were berry bushes and flowers in the yard. The place was beautiful. My Grandmother Spencer lived in a little house across the street.

Soon after I arrived, Superintendent H. M. Fulfer and other New Mexico District Council officials asked my parents to go pastor the church at Dora, seventeen miles south of Portales near the Texas-New Mexico border. They agreed to go. My two brothers and I went with them. We were not well received in Dora, because we were sent there by NMDC instead of being voted in. There was no furniture in the parsonage, so for the first night, we slept on the benches inside the church with songbooks for pillows. It got a little cold. We had charge of the first service in Dora on Sunday, September 1; there were twenty people present. Before long, the people loved us and the feeling was mutual. Mom and Dad took turns ministering the Word. Their messages were full of scripture, but different; one complemented the other. Dad's was centered on worship and Christian testimony. Mom had taken many Berean School Correspondence Courses, so she included more doctrine and prophecy. I organized music and youth activities. By teaching the teenage Sunday school class, I passed on to them what I had learned from William B. McCafferty and others at SBI. We established a prayer room that was used extensively by the youth. On weekdays, I helped a lady with Sunday school for the homebound.

Mr. Scott owned a local garage and attended church when he could. One day, he asked Dad to help him kill and dress a cow. Dad came home with a quarter of the beef and told us that Mr. Scott was planning a business trip to Phoenix. Mom and I decided to ask Mr. Scott if we could go with him, and he agreed. We had no idea what all was going on in Phoenix at the time! We went to visit Aunt Leonora's family, my former teletype peers and church friends at Eleventh and Garfield in Phoenix. When we arrived in Phoenix, we learned that my sister, Mae, and her new husband, Dave, had arrived in Phoenix from San Diego. That is the very first time we met Dave. Leonora and her husband, Nevin, had gone to Tucson. My teen-age cousin, Robert, phoned his parents in Tucson and said, "Come home! Relatives are coming through the windows and out of the woodwork." Leonora said, "Don't worry! Turn the beds and kitchen over to Edna; she always knows what to do." True, my mom could organize. I visited my former teletype peers in the Security Building. Unexpected things were also happening. The 1956 Arizona District Council was in session. The speaker was Reverend E. S. Williams, general superintendent of the Assemblies of God from Missouri. At a Youth For Christ rally, Reverend Steelburg was the speaker, Beverly Shea sang, "I'd Rather Have Jesus Than Anything," and Pat Zondervan talked about seeing the letters G-P in the sky and said he thought it meant *go preach*, when it must have meant *go publish*. On the front page of a book, which I have used to keep birth dates for forty-eight years, there is a note that reads, "In appreciation from Pat and Bernie Zondervan." They signed the book and sent it when I worked in the bookstore at SBI. On Saturday, Mom and I ate lunch with Mae Livengood and her mom and slept there Saturday night. Leonora and Nevin had come back from Tucson; beds were getting scarce. On Sunday morning, we attended First Assembly at Eleventh and Garfield Streets where the Loren Fox Party was in revival.

Mae and Dave left for Tucson on Monday morning to continue their belated honeymoon. They planned to stop in Dora to visit us before they returned to California. Dave was still in the U.S. Navy. That same day, Mr. Scott, Mom, and I headed for New Mexico. I did most of the driving. Mr. Scott was tired from business meetings. He insisted that I drive at least fifty miles per hour. I was not totally comfortable driving that fast, but we arrived safely. That was the start of my fast driving. An Indian once gave me a new name, "Leadfoot."

At a 1947 NMDC Spring Convention at Clovis, New Mexico, the executive committee granted me my first certificate of fellowship and license to preach with the Assemblies of God. It was signed by H. M. Fulfer and B. H. Caudle. Martha Roberts presented her plans to go to India as a missionary during that same convention. She and I had graduated from SBI on the same date. On the way back to Dora, Mom and Dad said they might loan their car for me to drive Martha on her itinerary around New Mexico. She had been depending on the pastors or a commercial bus line to get from one town to the next. We phoned Martha, and she gladly accepted.

One week after the convention, Reverend E. J. Stone, the New Mexico state DCAP (youth director), came to Dora church for an official visit with the youth group. He seemed impressed with their activities, level of dedication to Christ, increase in number, and enthusiasm. There were many young people in Dora and the surrounding small towns—the Wilchers, Scotts, Bateses, and others. The youth groups in Dora, Portales, and Clovis sometimes exchanged programs to share talents. While in Portales for National Youth Day, Reverend Henson helped us get a spare tire prepared for "Sally the Car" before Martha and I left for a month of meetings from March 10 to April 10, 1947. We met many pastors and their families and made new friends. When the San Jon pastors were not at home, we accidentally met Reverends

Vanzant and Stone, touring for youth and Sunday school departments; they told us to go to the Stemple residence. I learned why when I met with the Stemples that first of many times. They had a "prophet's chamber." Every evangelist or missionary with reason to be in San Jon stayed with them. At Capulin, we met ranchers Ola and Edna Johnson, Charlotte Smith's parents, for the first time. Lawrence and Nina Green were at Raton. In Santa Fe, we spent the night with Dovie Mae Nash, Gloria Gray, and Eddie Mae Rouse, friends who worked at the capitol. Wesley and Charlotte Smith were pastoring in Hatch with their new daughter, Margie. Nolan Smith, son of the Alamogordo pastor, had married Della just the day before we got there. Our twenty-seventh service that month was in Roswell, where Martha Roberts was usually called, "Little Martha." That was her home. I left Little Martha in Roswell at the home of Mr. And Mrs. George Clem, parents of Clifton Clem who teased Katherine and me about giving the itch to a cow at SBI.

I went home to Dora. Mom and Dad were happy to get their car back. They were starting a revival at the church with Evangelist Lane. On Saturday, they drove to Elida, eighteen miles directly west, to invite the Nunn family, who attended the Dora Church. Mom had always wanted to visit Elida, as her dad had bought a house there and moved it south on skids to Bronco, New Mexico, when she was ten years old. At Dora, we were living on the edge of her childhood home locations and traumatic memories. During the meetings, many people committing their lives to Christ and several Christians received the baptism in the Holy Spirit. I have pictures of Dad baptizing people near a bridge. I spent hours in the prayer room with young people. Lois Bates was receiving invitations to preach, even into Texas. She was a senior in Dora High School, along with my brother, Calvin Lee. Lola Bates, still in high school, was receiving regular invitations to sing. Willy Ruth Bates was in school at SBI in Waxahachie. I mailed her a cake on her birthday. Attendance increased in every department. We still were not receiving enough money from the church to feed a family of five. We supplemented; the laundry man in town brought loads of laundry for Mom and me to wash. For more food, Dad joined other ministers on deer hunts.

Grace Davis wrote from SBI that Fred Dudley lost his brother, James, in the horrible explosion in Texas City on April 16, 1946. Both were SBI students. Grace's letter sort of reminded me that summer was here; I must go back and complete the credits at SBI before I could go to Africa. I was so concerned about where I would get the money that I dreamed. In real life, I never had a job that involved food. However, in a dream, I was working at a fast food drive-in. All night, long I tried to get one hamburger to one customer; I never succeeded. I wrote to SBI about going back to summer school to finish the final credits needed on my transcript and I sent thirty dollars to finish paying the prior school debt. Within days, a reply came that I should come.

On May 11, 1947, Calvin, my brother, and Lois Bates graduated from Dora High School. Dad, as a local pastor, invoked God's blessing on the graduating class. After the exercises, Dad, Calvin, Lois Bates, and I left Dora about midnight and arrived at SBI about noon the next day. Lois stayed in the dorm with her sister, Willie Ruth, who was totally surprised to see her. Dad and Calvin slept two nights in the women's dorm sickbay for their motel. The students seldom used that room. Dad and Calvin sat with me in one of my classes taught by William Burton McCafferty. Dad presented his amazing testimony about the miraculous healing of his head. He, Calvin, and Lois returned to Dora. I went back to work in the bookstore. Students were clamoring for books, and the business office was clamoring for totals. Grace Davis, my boss, had a room in the girls' dorm. I decided to room with her as we could talk and plan our work and rent was cheaper. I studied in empty dorm rooms to allow Grace to sleep. When Grace took books to sell at conventions, I was excused from classes to be in the bookstore.

⌒

Martha Roberts visited SBI to bid her friends farewell, as she was on her way to India. On May 31, Martha and Willow Dean Deerman left to drive to New Mexico. Willow Dean was a sister to Willis Deerman, who was a very special minister in the New Mexico District. I never saw Martha again before she sailed to India. By then, people at SBI knew I planned to go to Africa. One day Professor Klaude Kendrick came into the bookstore. He loved to tease and lived to tease. He said, "I can just see you on a bicycle riding over the hot sands of Africa." We both laughed, but that is just exactly what did happen eventually!

When the summer session ended, students for that session went home. I was still working to pay off my school debt before I left; it took me almost until Christmas. Then, I resigned from the bookstore and Western Union downtown. When I finally left SBI for good, I received a handwritten letter on Christmas paper. It read, "Miss Charlese Spencer: We have appreciated your great help in the book store at Southwestern Bible Institute. We shall miss you when you leave. May the Lord bless you with many happy years in His service. We wish for you a Merry Christmas and a Happy New Year. (Signed:) M. E. Collins."

My feelings were quite ambivalent, both joy and stress. I thought, "My Bible school requirements for Africa are complete. What next?" In a room, on one of four bare mattresses on two bunk beds, I was taking an afternoon siesta. I wanted to be alone just to pray and think of my next step. I dreamed I was working at a dime store. While waiting on a customer, I reached under the counter to get a set of salt and pepper shakers. As I started to pull them out, a hand held them and my hand firmly. A voice said, "That is not what I want you to have. Ask of me, and I will give thee the heathen for thine inheritance." Psalms 2:8. I awoke. I was impressed that the salt and peppershaker was a pair—husband and wife or a son and daughter. I put on my blinders again; it was late in 1947. I went back to New Mexico.

Dad and Mom were still pastoring in Dora, but they resigned within a short time. They were accepted to pastor the Assembly at Dexter, near Roswell, and made many new friends again. My youngest brother, Royce, was still at home and in high school. I went by to help Dad build a parsonage for them, but I left before it was completed. On my way to live and work in Albuquerque, I stopped in Roswell to talk with Reverend and Mrs. Earl Vanzant about the possibility of my going to Africa as a missionary. I had known and respected them since their years of pastoring in Mountainair. They had known me as a young person in the New Mexico churches. It seemed important that, as district or sectional officials, they understand the reality of my call to Africa. If they had not thought about it before, I went away feeling that they believed in me. Their support in subsequent years proved that I was correct.

In Albuquerque, Mary Gray and Rae Elliott were living in the old parsonage behind First Assembly on North Second Street. They were on staff at the church. Rae Elliott had moved there from Phoenix and brought her two daughters, Wanda and Lulabelle. I stayed with them for a short time until the district officials sent Alma Spriggs, of Clovis, and me to Grants as interim pastors. We went, and I made more lifelong friends. After a time, the people voted in a permanent pastor. Alma returned to Clovis, and I went to Albuquerque to start looking for a job and teaching the college and career class in First Assembly Sunday school. I needed money for nurses training to get me to Africa. There was no need, in Albuquerque, for a teletype operator at Western Union. I took a bookkeeping job at Albuquerque National Bank. I moved away from my friends in the old parsonage and rented an apartment on Forester, NW. My brother, Calvin Lee, applied at the same bank and was hired as a bookkeeper, so we shared my apartment. Twice on Sundays and some week-nights, we walked eight blocks to church on North Second Street. On workdays, we walked over a mile to work at the bank on Second Street and Central. Our parents had moved to Belen, thirty miles south and had a thriving business.

I learned that the *only school of nursing* in New Mexico was right in town at St. Joseph Hospital. It was a three-year diploma program. I took an entrance exam at the University of New Mexico as the science classes were taught there. I talked with Sister Andrew, director of Regina School of Nursing. She said my score in math was impressive, and I was admitted to the school of nursing. In the fall of 1948, I quit my job at the bank and moved into Seaton Hall. I paid what money I had; it was not enough for even one full year. Sister Andrew said, "The probation period consists of the first six months. If at that time you are deemed to be nurs-ing material, we will talk about money." Apparently I was deemed—she talked with the Pilot Club of Albuquerque, and they gave me a loan scholarship. Money left from what I had paid six months prior was returned to me for spend-ing money to last me for more than two more years. On my birthdays and for holidays I received greetings with small gifts like a scarf or earrings from the Pilot Club. The club was a women's service club chartered from 1940 through 1993 as the Pilot Club International. One of the club's members, Mil-dred Stamps, was employed at Albuquerque National Bank from 1948 to 1974. She was there when my brother, Calvin Lee, advanced from a bookkeeper to become a teller and ul-timately an officer in that bank.

⌒

Few people knew that I planned to go to Africa. I had not told my local pastors, Paul and Lena Harrington. I did not talk to Sister Andrew or the Pilot Club ladies about Africa. I kept thinking that if I made a big issue of my plans to go to Africa and never got there, I would seem foolish. If I said nothing, and God wanted me there, He would get me there. I continued to teach the senior high school, college, and careers class in Sunday school as long as I was not yet doing clinical practice in the nursing program. When we started going to the hospital to care for patients, my hours were too uncertain. I had to give up teaching the Sunday school class. Not before, however, an incident occurred. Buster and Darrel Redfearn were in that class. They were from a family who owned the sweet shop where we young people liked to go for ice cream treats. Also in that class were twins, Jack and Jean Brock, who played football at UNM. With all my bible school training, they were a challenging group. I do not remember the context, but one Sunday while teaching I said, "Well, you know, the Bible says in Matthew 19:19 to be kind to your navel." Everything got deathly quiet for just one instant while I stood speechless. Then, all in unison, we roared with laughter. I tried to explain, "Anatomy in nurses training." Nothing helped. Someone in the class often give me a ride back to my dorm after church. If Jack, Jean, and their dates took me to my dorm, their humorous mom was along. She loved root beer, but if we stopped by an A&W Drive-In, she would point to the menu and say, "I want some of that root—." She would not even *say* the word "beer."

When we students were first assigned to patient care in the hospital, I was so frightened. I could feel the blood settling from my head. I stooped over, rolled up the head of a bed, lowered a bed, tied my shoe, untied my shoe, and retied my shoe—anything to get my head low when I felt the blood settling. This was soon overcome. I got so interested in the needs of the patients that I forgot myself. I thought that I would surely faint when I actually helped doctors operate. Think of all that blood! We had to stand on a little box for a better view of the surgical field so we could anticipate what surgical instrument the doctor might need or call for. I expected to faint and fall off that box. I never did; we were too busy. People were admitted with pain and serious illnesses.

We operated on them and saw them walk out with the problem solved. Instant gratification! Before long, I preferred surgery to medical or obstetrics. I did not tolerate pediatrics, where children were sick.

The time came when, with classes and clinical practice, I had little time for church. My brother, Calvin, married. I missed a bus, and so missed his wedding. Buster married Virginia that same day; I missed both weddings! Lois (Bates) from Dora and Cecil Holley got married in Texas and came to the school of nursing on their honeymoon. How great, but we barely had time to go grab a hamburger. Mary (Gray) Waldon married in Albuquerque in late October 1951, near the end of my junior year. For some reason, one of her sisters could not get there, and I became a stand-in member at the wedding.

At one point in our junior year, we students felt we were so overworked that we had a meeting and asked the officials and teaching sisters to hear us. We stated our case: "There were too many classes, too many hours on duty, too many heavy assignments, not enough hours in a day to do all this." Then it was their time to speak. Apparently, previous classes had survived. The school curriculum proceeded as scheduled! On an evening shift, one patient was recovering from spinal surgery; he was a doctor. I was in my senior year and in charge of a whole wing as salaried nurses wanted Sundays off. The pharmacy opened only at certain times on Sundays, so nuns could attend church. An orthopedic surgeon made his rounds and ordered a new pain medication for the spinal fusion doctor-patient. I could not get the medication immediately as the pharmacy was closed. Young Dr. Randy Lovelace came in to visit the doctor-patient. He came to the nurses' desk and demanded to know why we had not administered the new medicine ordered for pain. I told him the pharmacy hours; he told me to get the medication! When the pharmacy opened, I got the medication and gave it to the doctor-patient. He railed on me worse than Dr. Randy had. He told me that I had no business in nursing and that I should be *out on a farm pitching hay.* This student nurse in charge of a ward went into the utility room among the bedpans and cried, and then I went about my work. The next day, I reported the incident to Sister Andrew. I heard she really got after those doctors. A few weeks later, I was standing on the little box in surgery, slamming a forceps into the gloved palm of a doctor who was operating on a patient. At some point, the doctor looked over and recognized me. He was the doctor who had undergone the spinal fusion, and I was his nurse, the one that *should be pitching hay.* We completed the operation, and after we removed our caps and masks, he said, "You know that doctors and nurses are the most difficult patients. I just knew I would do some dumbfool thing when I went in for the surgery." We laughed.

While a student nurse, I became very ill with the same symptoms that I had experienced while going to high school in Hot Springs. I had not been taken to a doctor; we called the pastor to pray. We thought it was appendicitis. I recovered slowly. Now I was having the same symptoms ten years later. We students were especially fond of a certain doctor whose teenage daughter was dying of cancer. He was my doctor. Jokingly, he called my condition McKinnon's disease; that was his name. Finally, when my fever went dangerously high, I was taken to the emergency room. Dr. McKinnon did immediate exploratory surgery. The appendix was healthy, but he removed it and a gangrenous ovary that contained a ruptured dermoid cyst. There were tags in the area that seemed to show that it had been gangrenous at some previous time; that would have been in Hot Springs. The ovarian cyst contained teeth, nails, and hair; I was possibly meant to be twins. Two of my cousins have had something similar. In that experience, I discovered two things: Demerol sends me into shock and the sulfa drugs cause my temperature to spike to 104F degrees. Other antibiotics like penicillin were not yet available. Mom came from Belen and stayed with me in Seaton Hall while I recovered.

For our last year in nursing school, we seniors moved into Regina Hall across Grand Avenue. (That street is now Martin Luther King Jr. Boulevard, and an ophthalmology group has set up practice in that building. A friend of mine, Karen Hughes, once worked for them. The city considers the building historic and will not allow it to be torn down.) From Regina Hall we rotated to Nazareth Sanitarium for psychiatric training and then to Santa Fe for public health practice. Nazareth San was far north of Albuquerque at the time, but the city grew to include it long ago. We students were having difficulty getting from Nazareth to classes at St. Joseph Hospital on the bus, so Mom and Dad loaned me a little white car they had taken on a debt. We named it Casper and drew a picture of the Friendly Ghost on the side. A tin can was on the dashboard for all students to contribute gas money. One day, we drove into town and parked behind the hospital as usual. When we got out of class, Casper had *disappeared*. We hunted through the parking lot and found it had rolled down a hill and crashed into another car. Casper had lost the water from its radiator. The gas cap from the other car had flown through the air from the impact that crushed its left rear fender. Someone was watching us from an upper story window: the *hospital pathologist!* Casper had struck his car, so he came down. When he realized we were student nurses, he said, "Looks like you may have more problems than I have. You take care of yours; I'll take care of mine." We did. Winter got cold. Casper had no heater. Dad said, "Bring it down to Belen, I have an old heater to put in it." The heater didn't fit. Mom gave me some old quilts to throw over us. My roommate, Marion Holcomb from Gallup, and the other passengers teased me the rest of the winter by calling the quilts heaters. They worked, and we were grateful.

Finally, our group completed the course of study at Regina School of Nursing. We took the dreaded state board of nursing exams. If we did not pass, we went back for more schooling. We could not graduate from the school if we did not pass the state exams. While we waited for the results of the state board exam, I traveled to Springfield, Missouri. Noel Perkin was the director of missions for the Assemblies of God. H. B. Garlock was their African field representative. I told them I had gone through nursing school on a loan scholarship. They were kind, but said to return when I was free of debt. Two Regina students had averaged higher grades than I during the three-year curriculum. However, within a month, the results of our State Board Exam came, and I had scored top in the State of New Mexico. The day before our graduation, Mildred Stamps, representing the Pilot Club, phoned and said, "We have been told that you made top state board scores in your class. We are proud of our first sponsored nursing student, so we have decided you will not need to pay back the loan." One moment I owed for three years of training; the next moment I was free of debt. I mumbled something like, "Oh, mercy, you know I could have a heart attack to be told something like that over the phone." Then I expressed my sincere appreciation. I was in shock. The next day I graduated; I was an R.N. Mom and Dad came from Belen and seemed proud.

1. Book Store and manager, Grace Davis, helped pay my way. 2. A note of thanks for doing that. 3. Friends since 1941, the Kendricks. 4. Martha R. and I toured New Mexico. She went to India. 5-6 Calvin Lee worked with Mr. Gordon, maintenance engineer for SBI. 7. New Mexico friends, Lois B. and Mary G. , evangelists. 8. Outstation, clinical experience for students. Carl and Jewel Walker, pastors (once pastors at Hot Springs T or C, New Mexico). 9. My only sister married in San Francisco and 10. I graduated again—Bible and Missions 1956.

1. Magdalena, New Mexico, our first effort at evangelism. 2-4. Dora, first pastorate where we made friends forever. 5. Nostalgic visit back to Phoenix. 6. My first A/G ministerial license. 7-17. Itinerary with Martha Roberts in my parents' car, Sally. A wheel leaked brake fluid. Friends and new friends: Boyds at Clayton; Greens at Raton; Gloria Robin, Eddie Mae at Santa Fe; Jernigans in Albuquerque; E. E. Franks at Hot Springs; W. Smiths in Hatch; I. Smiths in Alamogordo. Nolen and Della Smith had married the day before, March 30. Martha went to India.

CHAPTER 8

# New Mexico, Pennsylvania, and Itinerary to England

M Y BLINDERS KEPT ME focused straight ahead. I phoned H. B. Garlock at the missions department in Springfield and asked, "Did I tell you I owed for my three years of schooling? Well, today I owe nothing." It had been less than a month since I talked with him. He could hardly believe me; it seemed like a miracle to both of us. I went to church and told my pastors, Paul and Lena Harrington, about my plans for Africa. They said, "You certainly did not advertise it." It was true that not many people knew. I told them that I had decided that I would do all I could to prepare. If I never went, no one but me would ever know I planned to go. I could always use the education, even America.

For a while, I worked as a registered nurse at St. Joseph Hospital. There were lots of memories in that one hospital: my young Uncle Roy and Grandpa Spencer from the train wreck; my dad with the fractured skull and other illnesses; my mom's surgery; me with the sewed up face from the wreck; and now, my first employment as an R.N. Nevertheless, I severed the umbilical cord and moved to Belen, where I was office nurse for Dr. J. A. Rivas. I planned to leave America soon and wanted to be near my parents before going away for years. Immediately, I became C.A president (youth leader) and Sunday school teacher for the senior high and career class in the Belen Church. Huletta, Mary Gray Waldron's younger sister, was in that class; we became life-long friends.

At Christmas time 1952, Dad, Mom, and I went to San Diego to be with my sister and family. We returned to Belen late in the night and slept. Early the next morning Dad shook me awake. At first I thought I had overslept and was due at the doctor's office. Dad said, "Mom is in the front room floor, and she does not respond." As I walked into the front room, I realized that I was staggering. I said, "Dad, it's gas; open all windows and call Doctor Rivas, my boss." I knew that he would advise Dad from there. I walked to the front door and opened it. When I inhaled fresh air mixed with the concentration of carbon monoxide gas, I lost consciousness. I plunged face-first down the front cement steps and out onto the snowy lawn clad only in my thin nightgown. When I awoke, the doctor was telling someone to get blankets and put me into the house. They put Mom and me into the same bed with an electric blanket to warm us. My face was scraped, and a dent across my forehead took months to heal. The local gas company had recently condemned the stove my parents had safely used for years. They compelled my parents to buy this new one, which was supposedly up to proper regulations; it almost killed us.

Mother Spencer had an apartment on the north end of my parents' house. She had developed hardening of the arteries and often wandered off in the night, so my parents placed her to sleep with me. This time, there was no feather bed. In the night she would say, "My teen-age friend, Maude, has left my coat at the door; I must go get it." I would need to go to the door with her to prove that there was nothing there. My sleep was interrupted, but more than that, my heart was sad to see my Mother Spencer like that. Her sister, Laura, died that February of 1953. When we recently passed through Phoenix, we had brought the news back that Dad's niece, Anne, had lost her husband that same month. All this added to my Mother Spencer's stress.

February 23, 1953, was my last day of work for Dr. Rivas. I was actually free for the first time in many years—after school, teletype, SBI, A. N. Bank, Regina, and Dr. Rivas. I really felt a loss. What a feeling of ambivalence. My freedom lasted *three whole days!* A letter arrived, calling me to the division of foreign missions in Springfield, Missouri. That night at a prayer meeting in the home of Oscar and Freeda (Gray) Galloway just north of Belen, Oscar said he would plan for the following Tuesday's youth service. Doyle and Lola (Bates) Wilson from the Dora church, agreed to take it the following Tuesday if I had not returned. The Wilsons, like my parents, had recently moved to Belen. The letter from DFM was my first concrete evidence that I had reached the impossible dream that I had nurtured for years. Since leaving my teletype job at the War Agency in Phoenix, I had worn blinders, like a team of horses, to keep me focused straight down the road and not be distracted on the sidelines. Activities and goals must lead me closer to Africa:

- Evangelism with Mary Gray Waldon—ever so short.

- Bible School graduate of 1946—completed in 1947.

- Became a licensed minister, New Mexico District 1947.

- Drove Mom and Dad's car through the whole New Mexico District for Little Martha Roberts; I knew most of the pastors.

- Co-pastored with Mom and Dad at Dora and Dexter.

- Co pastored with Alma Spriggs in Grants.

- Taught the college and career class in two Sunday schools.

- Completed Regina School of Nursing in 1952.

I had something to offer! The letter from H. B. Garlock said Helen R. Kopp and I were to meet the mission board in Springfield, Missouri on March 3, 1953. Helen was a nurse from Lancaster, Pennsylvania who, like me, had completed bible school and a nursing program and was willing to go to West Africa. Talk about timing. Things were moving rapidly. I was introduced to Helen Kopp in the office of Reverend Garlock on Monday. We met the board on Tuesday. Earnest and Martha (Roberts) Sherrick had met my bus when I arrived in Springfield. Martha had returned from one term in India and married Earnest, and they were in school to prepare to go to India together. While we were waiting for the results of our meeting with the mission board, Martha had a special dinner for us and invited Sketo, a friend from SBI, and Betty Snow, a friend from my home church in Albuquerque.

On Wednesday, March 4, Reverend Garlock and the mission board added three more huge goals: money, a physical, and midwifery in England:

1. "As soon as the necessary *cash* for your fare and equipment has been raised and you have pledges for your *monthly support* for at least three years, you will receive appointment.

2. Mrs. George Carmichael will help you receive *medical clearance* before you leave America.

3. The Gold Coast Government requires that those who operate an in-patient maternity clinic, without a doctor in residence, have a certificate of midwifery. We recommend you enter a school of midwifery in London *within 90 days*. May the Lord bless you. We have advised New Mexico District Superintendent Paul Holdridge of your being endorsed for appointment when the above stipulations are met.

Signed: H. B. Garlock, Secretary for Africa."

My reaction was: "What, in 90 days? How much money are you talking about?" The amount quoted seemed a phenomenal challenge. "More school? No, I've gone to school all my life. If you want me as-is, I am ready. Otherwise, I will go with another mission board." Finally, I agreed to try. None of us seemed to know there was a Catholic school of midwifery in Santa Fe, New Mexico, just sixty miles from my home. That is really where professional midwifery in the USA was born. It was best, however, that we have British-oriented midwifery since the Gold Coast of West Africa was British influenced. In the early morning of March 4, Helen and I left Springfield by Greyhound bus. The next morning at 8:40 A.M., we arrived in Albuquerque, New Mexico and prepared visual aids, and at 2:00 P.M., presented our plan at a spring convention. It was held at West Mesa Assembly of God, where Wesley and Charlotte Smith and family were pastoring. Things were definitely speeding up.

The New Mexico District Council (NMDC) was holding its spring conventions, and missionary conferences were being held simultaneously during the month of March. H. Paul Holdridge, district superintendent, and Ted Vassar, veteran missionary to India, were traveling over New Mexico for those meetings. The Vassar family had been in India the same time as Martha Roberts-Sherrick, whom I chauffeured all over New Mexico in 1947. I booked meetings for Helen Kopp and me with pastors of churches throughout New Mexico during that spring convention. My brother, Calvin Lee, was still working at the bank where we once worked together in bookkeeping. He took Helen and me about thirty miles south from the conference to Belen, my home since leaving the school of nursing. Helen and I washed clothes and prepared to travel over New Mexico. On Sunday, March 8, we presented our plans in the Belen Assembly, my latest home church. My dad and mom loaned me their car again for the trip around New Mexico. It was a lovely two-tone Pontiac with overdrive, a far cry from Sally, which I drove for Little Martha.

Reverend Holdridge and Reverend Vassar went on their way to sectional spring business conventions in March with four services on specific days. Helen and I met them at those conferences held in the four corners of New Mexico: On March 5, they were with Pastor W. Smiths at West Mesa Assembly in Albuquerque; on March 10, they were at First Assembly in Tucumcari; on March 13, they were with Pastor R. Stewart at First Assembly in Clovis; on March 26, they were at the Deming Assembly where the Bubbs pastored. They allowed us to present our plans and need in the 2:00 P.M. service and book appointments with pastors in towns for every night. Churches were giving cash for travel fare to England and Africa and for equipment. They were pledging five to fifteen dollars per month for support. We especially enjoyed the pastors' children. Doyle and Dolores Chaney were in Mountainair; Eugenia and Buddy Stewart were in Clovis.

On March 13, 1953, a phone call found us in Clovis. My Mother Spencer had died. We continued as scheduled with the evening service in Clovis. We left just before midnight to return to Belen to be with my family. The funeral was in Mountainair the following day. Because of this, Helen was able to meet my other brother, Royce Ray. He was given leave from the navy to come to the funeral. After the funeral, Helen and I went back to the east side of the state to continue our schedule at Fort Sumner, Melrose, and Texaco. In Portales, Reverend and Mrs. Earl Vanzant were pastors; we met their younger sons, Homer and Larry. Their older children, Clinton, Thurman, Velma, and Carl, whom I had known for years, had already left the nest. After those services, we went south to Dexter, Hagerman, and Lovington. The Botelers in Lovington had several children. The Raymond Hudsons were pastors at First Assembly in Hobbs. They graduated from Southwestern Bible College about the time I graduated from Southwestern High School in Fort Worth. The Reverend Roy F. George family were pastoring at Hobbs Glad

Tidings Assembly. Their two young sons, R. Kenneth and J. Don, were already flexing their preaching muscles.

The spring convention in Deming was on March 26. After we made our presentation, we were invited to eat a Mexican dinner at the home of Fred and Bonnie Chambers. One of their twin daughters was there; the other was away at school. The local pastors, Reverend and Mrs. Bubb, and the two visiting ministers, Holdridge and Vassar, were invited too. Bonnie rode with Helen and me to show us the way to their home out on a huge farm. The long lovely dining table was laden with everything to make enchiladas, tacos, or any dish we New Mexicans love. Helen Kopp had never seen this kind of food in Pennsylvania. She liked it until—I looked at her just as she bit into a whole Jalapeno pepper! She said she thought it was a pickle. The tears flowed and nothing could cool the fire. Mexican cafés were off-limits for the rest of our tour.

The Irving Smiths were pastors at Silver City. They still had three children at home: Milton, Berniece (Mrs. Pete Pelletier) and Florence (Mrs. Joe Robinson). Glen and Peggy Anderson were pastors at the other church in Silver City. They had Barbara (Andy) in school, and John, who was yet pre-school. Glen was New Mexico District Christ ambassador president (DCAP). We met Kenzy and Esther Savage's youngest daughter, Patsy, and her husband in Silver City. They were looking forward to missionary work in Latin America. Patsy's older sister, Bobbie (Savage) Wheeler had been married for some time. One morning Helen, and I went with the Andersons and several of their church lay people, including Jim Trewern's parents, high into the mountains of the Gila National Forest to cook breakfast of bacon and eggs over a camp fire.

In Las Cruces, we watched teenagers Buster and Steve Deerman be baptized in the Rio Grande River by Pastor E. E. Franks. The Franks had one daughter. There we met teenagers Dale and Ray Franks. Their parents were R. L. and Mary

(Grubbs) Franks, pastors and church building contractors. In Roswell, we stayed in the home of Mr. and Mrs. George Clem, Little Martha's adopted parents. Mr. Click did some car repair for me again. He had done some on my car, Sally, when Little Martha and I arrived in Roswell in 1947. Paul and Ruth Savage were pastors at First Assembly in Roswell. They had pre-teens Beverly and David. At one town, we were placed to spend the night with an elderly saint just outside the city limits. I preferred homes to motels. Before retiring, she instructed us how to get to the two-seater up a little hill. She said, "Just feel for the clothes line at the corner of the house and hang onto it. It will lead you directly there!" Helen and I shared our very first pledge; we would not go there alone in the middle of the night.

The Artesia pastors were Reverend Howard and Wilma McClendon. Wilma's younger sister, Willie Tom Hunter, had graduated from high school with me at SBI. Their older sister, Thelia, was known for her music. The women of the churches in Artesia and Carlsbad gave me a huge set of stainless steel cookware. The McClendons and some of their church members took Helen and me out to a junkyard to practice shooting tin cans. I had hunted with Dad; Helen had never shot before but she hit the tin can on her first shot. The local youth leader in the Artesia church, Melvin Lloyd, who later married Ruby Whitehead, gave me the practice 0.22 rifle to take to Africa. Ruby and Viola Whitehead were an evangelistic sister team. I had also known them at SBI in 1942. Viola eventually married Grant Croasman from a family I had known in Hot Springs, New Mexico. They became missionaries to the Indians and had the famous display of Christmas lights near Grants, New Mexico, that could be seen from Interstate 40 (Route 66).

When Helen and I finally had a day of rest, we walked through the Carlsbad Caverns. Although I was born in New Mexico, I saw this awesome wonder for the first time with Helen. Our last meeting in New Mexico was at the First Assembly in Albuquerque, my home church while I was in nurses' training. From there, Helen left to be with her family in Pennsylvania for Easter, possibly the last time for four years. After Easter, I rode a Greyhound bus to Pennsylvania to help Helen raise her funds as she had done for me in New Mexico. The old cigarette smoke and exhaust fumes on the bus, combined with a reaction to a recent vaccination for smallpox, made me ill most of the way. My ears closed; I could not hear. I was young and slept a lot, so by the time I reached Lancaster, I was much better. I met Helen's dad, mom, brothers, sisters, nieces and nephews. Their tables of food were unbelievable, usually having a choice of meats and deserts.

Helen's district officials had helped her map out an itinerary. A man loaned her a car from his used car lot; I drove. Helen ordered a learner's permit and had it sent to a pastor on down our scheduled itinerary. She practiced on country roads and schoolyards. One day, we were on a schoolyard for Helen to practice gear shifting and hand signals. We saw a police car approaching, so we quickly switched seats. The police followed us all the way to the parsonage, but they went on by. Her permit was waiting at the next church. She finished learning *on the Pennsylvania Turnpike*. We got one violation ticket that I still have—for parking on the street after 3:00 A.M. At the police station, we said that we were sorry and that we had parked there in the dark and had not seen the sign. The police chief signed the ticket, passed it around for other autographs and presented it to us. He said, "Thanks for not telling us how to run our town." Snow began to fall as we drove up a high mountain to a church in a mining town. When we arrived, the pastor was at a phone booth trying to locate us and advise us not to come. The place was beautiful, but we definitely were snowbound. We helped the pastor paint the church and his wife do the family wash. We wore boots to wade in knee-deep snow to hang heavy blue denims on a line. They froze stiff instantly. With all of this, we did not cancel one service scheduled.

We met the financial stipulations of our foreign missions board within March, April, and May, ninety days. I left Helen in Lancaster to pack. Our schedule was getting tighter, so I took my very first airplane flight ever. It was via American Airline to St. Louis, Missouri. The Ozark Commuter (affectionately spelled backwards by the Missouri people) took me south to Springfield. Because of the popularity of Branson, I suspect that process of getting to Springfield has changed long ago. I did not like flying; I still prefer my feet on terra firma. "In a car, if you crash, there you is; in a plane, if you crash, where is you?"

In DFM, Noel Perkin and H. B. Garlock were delighted with our financial report. They could proceed with our enrollment for midwifery in London. From Springfield, I rode a bus on to Waxahachie, Texas, where I was scheduled to speak on mission's day in the chapel at SBI on May 13. After I spoke, they pledged to buy the bicycle that I would need in Africa. Professor Klaude Kendrick could now be assured that I would *cycle over the hot sands of Africa* as he teasingly predicted.

I returned to pack in New Mexico, through June and July. My pastors in Albuquerque, Paul and Lena Harrington, allowed me to pack in their garage. Their daughter, Louise, had married and now lived out of town. Paul, Jr., their son, was in school at SBI. Mother Harrington, the pastor's mother, helped us pack. Frank Powers, a carpenter, made lumber crates to fit several cases of canned fruit, meat, and vegetables. His wife, Louise, started a scrapbook of my journeys. Their two teenage daughters, Geralda and Barbara, helped me pack to live in Africa for three years. A wood stove, springs and mattress, linen, clothing, medicine, and food would be stored for over a year in a New York warehouse until we were successful in our school of midwifery in London. Oscar and Freeda Galloway, and my mother, encouraged the Belen church to add a gasoline washing machine to the waiting freight.

Lena Harrington and Louise Powers took me to the train depot on July 10 and bade me farewell for four years. Dad had undergone recent surgery, and Mom had to be with him. Later, they sent me a *Belen Bulletin*, a daily paper, with an article and a photograph about my leaving and my overseas plans. The train sped me straight east across the United States to visit Mae, Dave, and their four-year-old, Jimmy, in Norfolk, Virginia. My brother-in-law, Dave, was still in the Navy. They took me to visit Williamsburg, a beach on the Atlantic Ocean, the Capitol in D.C. and other historic sites. At a cemetery in front of an old church, a sign read, "Here Lies America's Finest." Dave's one-liner was, "Hmm, I wondered where they were." My sister suggested that I take a ferryboat up the coast to New York for a change. The date was fast approaching for my sailing to England. Jimmy was my only nephew; I had no nieces. He gave me his olive drab, army-surplus, windup record player to take to Africa. We said our farewell. As I boarded the bus that was to take me to the ferry, Dave held my nephew, Jimmy, up to kiss me through the bus window. The memory of that kiss surfaced often over the next four years.

The trip from Norfolk to New York was the longest trip I had ever taken on a boat. It was pleasant. While in New York, I stayed on Summit Avenue in the Bronx at a house called Mizpah, meaning: "The Lord watch between us while we are absent one from another." Missionaries stayed there on arriving or departing. From Mizpah, I could walk past the awesome Yankee Stadium to a New York subway station and go anywhere in the city. Reverend Robert McGlassen had been placed in a New York City office by the foreign missions department to assist missionaries arriving and departing the United States. He presented me with a letter dated July 17, 1953, from Reverend Noel Perkin: "We are very happy to forward herewith your certificate of appointment and fellowship as a missionary of the General Council of the

Assemblies of God to the Gold Coast. In granting this appointment, it is understood that you are not being employed by the Assemblies of God but are going forth in obedience to what you believe is a call of God. We prefer not to designate a special term of years, it being considered that you are entering missions for life. A furlough will be considered after three years. Let us know if at any time you feel our advice might be of value, or we can help you in prayer; this will be a privilege."

Reverend McGlassen gave me a To Whom It May Concern letter: "Our organization assumes the full responsibility for the travel expenses of Miss Spencer, her maintenance while in England and in Gold Coast, and guarantees the cost of her repatriation whenever this may be required." It gave me a lonely feeling. They had been through this with so many; they knew how it worked. Helen said it was sort of like, "Here is your Bible and mosquito net; have at it!" They could never have written those letters without the support of our home districts. I carried a letter signed by Paul A. Shaver, Albuquerque chief of-police: "... no criminal charges pending against her at the present. Dated May 23, 1953." Was I a man without a country, a refugee, a fugitive, missionary, or all of the above?

We had made it! Packing had made it a bit over ninety days as stipulated on March 4. In about four months we had raised our total budget for the next fourteen months in a British midwifery school and three years in the Gold Coast of West Africa. The money was safely deposited with our mission headquarters in Springfield, Missouri. We felt rather proud of our families, friends, the churches in our respective districts, and ourselves. We sent cards to family and friends with a tentative address at King's College Hospital, London, England.

On Monday, July 20, 1953, I stood on the deck of the *Veendam*, a luxury liner of the Holland-American Line. The night before at Mizpah, I slept restlessly. Reverend McGlassen had arrived at 5:00 A.M. to drive me through the Lincoln Tunnel to Hoboken, New Jersey. The *Veendam* was docked at Pier Five. Helen's family had brought her from Lancaster that morning. Her sisters, Janet and Mary, and her brother, Paul, were there with some of their children: Jimmy, LeVan, and Patty. When I saw them saying farewells, I was almost glad all mine were behind me; it was so emotional. I was grateful that Reverend McGlassen stayed with us until visitors must leave the ship. What a sight. All the people left behind were waving, laughing, and weeping as we on the *Veendam* slowly slid away from Pier Five at high noon. The outline of the Statue of Liberty appeared, and we glided smoothly by. What a feeling of nostalgia mixed with anticipation, as The Lady again faded into the fog.

I asked myself, "Did I really get this done?" I had to say again, I've come a long way, baby! I was far from the three-cornered house in Mountainair. I even thought about the roses I still had not found. Helen and I suggested we pinch each other to be sure we were for real; we had a long, un-known road ahead. When we located our stateroom, there were bouquets of flowers and boxes of candy waiting for Helen. She took the flowers to the dining room and shared the candy with passengers for days. The ocean was calm, but by evening some passengers were seasick. I was not. All my life I had suffered from nausea if I rode in the back seat of a car. I was pleasantly surprised to find a large ship did not affect me that way. People calling the ship a Dutch luxury liner overwhelmed me; I saw it as useful. A steward knocked on the door of our stateroom, number 458 B on the D deck. He had come to turn the covers on our bunk beds open for the night. I knew it was his job, but I wanted to say, "Don't do this again. I'm not a passenger on the ship; I'm just a person on my way to obey God. As student midwives, we will be making beds for others in a few days." For the moment, we tried to enjoy every new incident.

After two whole days, we kept seeing land, so we checked

the bulletin board that plotted our course and position. We had been going north, past Boston and Nova Scotia toward Newfoundland. I sent a radiogram from the ship to Mae and Dave to say we had indeed departed. In a wave of nostalgia, I realized that my nephew, Jim, would probably be nine years old when I saw him again. On the third day, we suddenly turned east to cross the Atlantic Ocean. We met a ship going toward America. One ship going east, as we were, passed us like we were dead in the water. We were told it was the new *Queen Elizabeth II*. I sent information to Dave and Royce about our fast ship. Being sailors, they might appreciate it. The *Veendam* was thirty years old. It had made 192 voyages with only two more to go. It was to be retired because the engines were slowing down. We were only traveling about 350 miles a day—no wonder I was not seasick. We met a nurse from Switzerland on board and a Rev. and Mrs. Rendel, Baptists, going to Nigeria. On Sunday, he spoke in an informal church service. On Sunday evening, Mr. Randolph Symonette, an opera singer, sang for the passengers in the dining room. It was fabulous. We had itinerated so fast that this was what we needed. One day a group of porpoises appeared and went jumping high out of the water alongside the ship as if saluting. Finally, on the second Wednesday at sea we discovered land. The captain's party took place that evening. We had been on board long enough to make several friends. Last minute pictures were taken with the Rendels, our roommate, Claire, and her husband. We were intrigued that she and her husband couldn't have a room together because of some classification of passengers.

Thursday morning, July 30, we awoke to find our ship was anchored in Cowes Roads near the Isle of Wight. British customs officials came on board and checked the luggage of all those disembarking. Helen, with her guitar, and I, with my accordion, record player, and other luggage, were helped onto a tender, which sped us to Southampton. We had not convinced our legs that we were on dry land before we were swaying on a fast train north to Waterloo Station in London. Vegetation was so green and lush that, compared to New Mexico, it was shocking. At Waterloo we found a taxi. Another shock! We could not understand the taxi driver, or he us, and we were all three supposedly speaking English. We had to show him the address in writing. We did not dare back-seat drive as he was driving on the wrong side of the street and we had no idea where the fast approaching vehicles were going or supposed to be. The driver stopped to ask the way, and the person answering him sounded like, "Hei, ye shud ha' tuined soo it 'd mine ooi." We learned he said, "Hey, you should have turned south at the fork of the main street." The driver got us safely to Coniston Lodge on Tyrwhitt Road (pronounced Tirit). Mr. and Mrs. C. P. Hubble were in charge. While we were at Coniston Lodge, Reverend and Mrs. Friesen and their two daughters, Gwen and Lois, arrived from America en route to the Belgian Congo. We visited. We listened. We learned a lot from them in a short time.

⌒

The ten-day voyage got us to London a few weeks after Queen Elizabeth II was crowned on June 2, 1953. I was surprised to find that the archbishop of Canterbury (clergy) placed the St. Edward Crown upon her head at the God-honoring coronation ceremony. Then, she was escorted to the throne by bishops (clergy) and temporal lords (politicians?). After this, she was eligible to wear the magnificent Imperial Crown set with some of the most famous jewels in the world. They are often displayed at the Tower of London. Beautiful decorations were still evident every place we traveled and especially in London. News reports on the royal children, Charles and Ann, were delightful!

Early Friday morning we reported to King's College Hospital for an interview with Matron, A. Opie. We were tentatively accepted for midwifery training and would receive an allowance of twenty dollars per month, the same as British pupils. We chose not to take the monthly allowance from our precious funds stored at DFM until we completed midwifery training. We might need it more in Africa.

We were measured for green denim uniforms under white, starched bib-aprons. Necessity taught us the London tube system in one day. We went back to Waterloo Station to have our stored luggage hauled to King's College Hospital. We visited Piccadilly Circus (circle). We shopped in the rain on Oxford Street in London Town to buy black shoes and stockings as part of our required uniform. When we asked directions we were told, "A five-minute walk and across the road." This caused us to anticipate an unpaved stretch of road somewhere ahead, but we discovered that even the broadest avenue was referred to as a road. In crossing these roads, we were careful to look both ways, only to step off the curb in front of a speeding taxi. We knew they drove on the left side of the street, but our brain had not assimilated this fact into our reflexes. Other cultural shocks included the language barrier, the sheer joy of being there, the anticipation of a strange educational system among non-American classmates, and shopping in unfamiliar stores for shoes with strange size markings while using unfamiliar money and rushing to meet a deadline. The drastically different climate forced us to buy overshoes and umbrellas first, but we were already soaked to the skin.

We bought programs of the Coronation of Her Majesty Queen Elizabeth II for ourselves. We bought souvenir tea trays containing pictures of the elaborate celebrations for Christmas gifts for family and friends in America. Other chores were:

> Go to the undersecretary of state at High Holborn, London, W.C.1., to register as aliens. We each got a letter stating: "After consultation with the ministry of labor and national service, the secretary of state has decided to allow (Spencer and Kopp) to stay in the United King-

dom for the purpose of midwifery training." Our passports were stamped accordingly.

Go to the general nursing council to become certified nurses and to the central midwives board to be accepted on the register of pupil midwives.

Get a permit to purchase the registered uniform prescribed by the General Nursing Council of England and Wales. (This was granted to us, so we could wear the denim and apron.

On the way back to the hospital, we rode on the top deck of a big, red London bus. At the intersection of Elephant and Castle, we saw a bombed-out shell of a beautiful church. A sign read, "Spurgeon's Tabernacle." Someone volunteered more information, "They still have church services in the basement." Many stately buildings stood only as shells, and whole city blocks lay in rubble from bombs. It sometimes brought tears to our eyes. We stashed our purchases in our rooms at King's College Hospital and returned to Coniston Lodge to get our belongings and check out. Back at the hospital we ate in the dining room where the menu read, "American Dry Hash." We unpacked, placed a padlock in the hasp on each drawer; that requirement was strange to us. We fell into bed and bounced off—it was Saturday.

Over the weekend, we were oriented to the physical facilities of hospital, classrooms, and post office. Letters from my parents and a package from my sister, Mae, were waiting. Helen had post too. We met our classmates from India, Ireland, Scotland, Africa, and England. They declared the midwifery program, "Shocking!" Some were self-proclaimed homosexuals. In America the topic was more covert, but Helen and I had discussed the subject before we left home. Neither was willing to spend the next four years with a lesbian as a co-worker. I wrote home to confirm my address: P.M. Elsie Charlese Spencer, King's College Hospital, Nurses Home, Denmark Hill, London, SE 5, England. P.M. meant Pupil Midwife. I was a student again.

In 1942, I had first obtained a ration book in America for butter, sugar, and meat and surrendered it to SBI cafeteria. Tires, gasoline, shoes, hosiery, and other items were limited to us in America during WWII. We thought times were hard, but all that had ended about 1946. Now, as pupils in 1953, we obtained a ration book and gave it to the cafeteria for butter and sugar again. The other pupil-midwives verbalized their delight that white pepper was available again as they were forced to use black pepper during the war. That brought back memories of WWII days in San Francisco when we were forced to use white pepper and suffered waiting for black pepper.

CHAPTER 9

# Midwifery:
# London and Surrey County

CLASSES STARTED MONDAY, AUGUST 3. Helen and I wrote frantically and phonetically, just how it sounded to us. Each evening we transcribed our notes together and tried to decide what the tutors had said; we were almost certain it was not English. Gradually, we understood better; finally, we wondered why we had not understood in the first place.

By Thursday, I had become so ill with a chest cold that I was put into the hospital as a patient. This dry-land New Mexican could not tolerate wet, cold London. The soaking we got while hunting black shoes and stockings down on Oxford Street had chilled me to the bone. My lungs hurt, and I was coughing. I could not eat. Someone brought me a London newspaper. The headline read, "Temperature Rises to a Record 88, while London Swelters." Here I was in the hospital with pneumonia from getting my footsies damp. We phoned Coniston Lodge to tell the Hubbles that we could not go to church with them on Sunday as planned. On the following Monday, I was discharged to my dorm room. I took a walk down the street to a lovely little park called Camberwell Green. At a little shop, J. Lyons & Co. Ltd., I ordered a cake with blue icing decorated with the words Happy Birthday Helen. It cost sixteen shillings, less than two dollars, and they delivered it August 20.

When I was feeling better, I went on duty in a ward. As I was weighing one of the post-partum mothers, I discovered that I did not understand the scales. She weighed eleven stone, two pounds. I hated to ask someone how to read a scale, but I did. A stone is fourteen pounds; she weighed one hundred and fifty-six pounds. Hey, I liked that; I couldn't wait to use those little numbers on myself.

One day, the weather cleared enough that I looked out my fourth floor dorm window and discovered multiple chimneys atop houses. Looking through and beyond those hundreds of chimney pots I could see Big Ben at the Houses of Parliament. We crossed a bridge over the River Thames near that point or walked along the Embankment parallel to the river many times during our fourteen months in England.

We first had to learn titles on our shifts of duty. The matron is the top authority, like a director of a hospital or college of nursing. A nursing sister is next in authority; it does not refer to any religious order. Matron or Sister must be addressed as such. The staff nurse does the hands-on nursing care, or makes sure that the pupil midwife who is lowest in the hierarchy, does it. Both staff and pupil could be addressed as "Nurse (Name)," as we were registered nurses before we could be pupil midwives. Highly qualified surgeons were addressed as Mister, as those addressed as doctor were a lower order.

One day a doctor asked, "Where is Sister?" Staff said, "Sister has gone to the theatre." I quickly asserted, "This is a fine time for Sister to go to a movie, we have a pregnant woman in convulsions!" The look on their faces said they did not understand my problem—forget the solution! Staff said, "Nurse Spencer, bring a trolley." The only trolley I knew was the one I rode up the hills in San Francisco's Chinatown to our flat on Hyde Street. I quickly learned and returned with a stretcher on wheels, a gurney, a cart, —trolley! We put the little mother on the trolley, and off they went with her. One evening as I was going off duty to my dorm room, I noticed signs above a group of doors in a hospital hallway: Theatre No. One, Theatre No. Two, and on up to five. I did know about operating rooms with seats for observation and teaching purposes, so now I knew Sister had gone to the operating theatre to prepare for a possible Caesarean section. It was too late for me to explain. The toxemia patient did have the Caesarean. When we discharged her, she was told to return to her Physician's Surgery for a two-week checkup. That is where he consults or clinically examines outpatients who have appointments. We Americans know it as the doctor's office.

One mother had just given birth and I was helping to care for her. She had massive, heavy, war scars on her body. Many of the women had them. Some talked about it if asked. At first, I was saddened and mesmerized, but when it gradually became commonplace to me, I felt a bit guilty. Along with learning midwifery, I was learning what war could do on your own home turf. (We learned a lot more when it reached the USA on September 11, 2001.) A voice brought me back to reality. Staff Nurse said, "Nurse Spencer, bring an aluminum bottle for this woman." The lady was shivering. Helen had warned me; it had already happened to her. In the utility room there was indeed a supply, my first encounter with aluminum hot-water bottles. Then Staff said, "Nurse Kopp, you go do the sluicing." Helen asked, "And where shall I go to do this?" There was that look again! "Well, to the sluice room, of course," she snapped. Neither of us knew where she was to go or what she was to do when she got there. We knew how to collect soiled linen after a delivery and send it down a laundry chute. We never sluiced the worse soil out prior to sending it down the chute. We did it many more times in England. These semantics were making us reinvent the wheel of basic nursing. Like Demerol, used in the delivery room for pain control, it was called Pethadine. In some of our humorous learning processes we laughed, *if they did!* In high stress situations, there was nothing humorous about it, and our learning could be dangerous as it took precious time. However, we rationalized, "This will help when we get to the British Gold Coast of West Africa." In September, we were oriented enough to be assigned to night duty from 8:00 at night to 8:00 in the morning—twelve hours. The cafeteria served us breakfast just before we went on duty for the night, lunch at midnight and a meal when we got off in the morning.

When teatime came, I hid in the utility room. I did not drink coffee with nurses in America, and I did not want tea with nurses in England. The Staff or Sister sent someone to find me and ask if I were ill. I started drinking tea to save them the trouble of hunting me. In time, they thought these two Americans should have a go at making tea. We did. Their comments are unprintable, and we were not asked to make tea again.

⸎

We finally found a Sunday we could visit the Hubbles and go to church with them. There we met a young man, named Benny, from Nigeria, West Africa. While working the night shift, we visited many of the attractions in and around London in the daytime. We saw Windsor Castle, Westminster Abbey, and the Houses of Parliament. We visited St. Paul's Cathedral, Madam Tausaud's Wax Exhibition, Tower Bridge, and the Tower of London, where we saw the crown jewels. There we saw the crown worn by Queen Elizabeth in the coronation just two months prior. After each trip, we returned to our dorm in time to sleep some before reporting for night duty.

Also on our off time, some of our classmates asked us

to teach them some American folk songs. They especially asked for "Home On The Range." Helen played the classical method on her guitar. I could chord on her guitar or my accordion when we gathered in a pupil midwife's room to sing. They loved the gospel songs of Ira Stanphill; his parents attended my home church in Albuquerque, New Mexico. It was not uncommon to be walking down a smoggy hallway in the dormitory or hospital and hear some pupil midwife singing, "I've got a mansion just over the hilltop," with a British accent.

A letter from my Aunt Leonora said that she was working in Wyoming's Yellowstone Park for the summer. That sounded exciting and much warmer than where we were. We must have convinced someone back in America how cold we were, and winter had not even arrived. Warm pajamas arrived from ladies in the Alamogordo church and a sweater came from Hobbs. A wool skirt came from a Silver City church—probably from Pennington's Store. Candy and two blouses came from my home church in Albuquerque, with a note from Lois Raines attached. I also needed some chili to help warm me. We had found a place in London to go for Chinese food, and a student from India prepared a curry dish one day. That was the best substitute I had found, but I was hungry for Mexican food. I wrote to friends in New Mexico about this serious need. The word spread, and Hatch green chili soon arrived and lifted my spirits considerably. Helen's memory of biting into the jalapeno pepper in Deming was dimming, and she developed a taste for Mountain Pass green chili scrambled with eggs in London. We had limited kitchen facilities. Occasionally, we were invited out to British homes to eat. Once, we were asked by two nursing tutors to have a meal with them. They lived in a house that, years ago, had been a private home. Now however, they taught fundamentals of nursing and were provided living quarters in that same house. Many large homes with winding staircases had been seized for taxes and used for government purposes. After visiting a bit, we sat down to a lovely meal. They asked us if we noticed anything different. We didn't. In exasperation, they said, "We spent hours hunting in exotic food stores for a tin of corn, and you do not even notice it!" Somehow it had slipped our mind that they did not have Indians to teach them to eat corn, on or off the cob. Our hosts said, "We only feed it to our stock." They felt better when we truly enjoyed the corn. It dawned on us that it had never been served in the hospital cafeteria.

In October, we were told the second three months of our training would be south of London at Redhill County Hospital, Earlswood Common, in Surrey County. One weekend, Helen and I took a beautiful ride on a train to locate our *future digs*. It was getting colder every month in London. Smoke from all the chimneys, mixed with fog, made heavy smog, even in the hospital and dorm halls. When we blew our nose, it was as if we had come from a coal mine. We looked forward to our time in the countryside; the smog would be less than in London. By the last half of October, we were starting to pack. Exams for the first three months of midwifery were beginning. I learned that instead of cramming for exams, in England we swatted. On the October 30, our test results returned; I tied for second place. On the last day of October, we worked until 2:00 P.M. and then moved to Redhill by train. Our group of six was P.M.s Gillett, Hall, Villiers, and Williams and Helen and I. What a sight! We had two guitars, one accordion, a wind-up record player, and a number of various shaped bundles, bags, and suitcases. We drew stares, comments, and questions, especially when they learned that two were Americans. A taxi sped us the last short lap from Reigate to Redhill Hospital; it was getting dark. Our rooms were cold, and in the darkness they seemed gloomy. We went on duty the next morning at 8:00 A.M.

At Kings College Hospital, we were observers and helped with deliveries. Here we would be delivering babies while someone supervised us closely. I was second in rotation to deliver a baby. It happened at two in the morning on November 3, when little Elizabeth presented herself to a very happy mother and new midwife. What a thrill! My diary says, "I thought I would be terrified; I was calm as a cucumber." That was the first of my hundreds of deliveries over the years. I assisted the next lady in the use of gas and air as a mild analgesic-anesthesia, while some other pupil midwife delivered her. The woman was on her side and held the mask herself; it must not be propped. When she got enough gas and air to relax, the mask fell away. My second delivery was one week later. I usually prayed as we anticipated the first shriek; the wonder never faded. Every baby has a specific personality from that first cry. Mother and infant stayed in the hospital twelve days, long enough for us to become attached to the pair. Doing what we came for became enjoyable.

At night in our dorm we nearly froze; it was stark winter. I bought a little electric heater. We drank strong British hot tea and studied in the bed under a pile of covers. We slept with hot water bottles. We took few baths. The tub had a heavy line painted inside about three inches from the bottom to tell us not to fill it above that line. When we were on duty, we wore a slip-on sweater under our denim uniform and a cardigan on top of that. At times, I wore a T-shirt and long legged cotton drawers under all that. We went around closing windows; they went around opening them. In the nursery, we bathed the babies with the windows up. No wonder Roger Miller wrote in his song about England, "The rosy red cheeks of the little children." In their perambulator (pram), they were placed outside daily for air in front of their apartment, even in the dead of winter. Their blood must have been as thick as molasses. Because of the terrorists around the world, I doubt that parents place them outside today.

Many of our classmates were saving their monthly allowance for some goal, like a visit to America. One day, I went downtown in London with two of them. I treated them to tea that cost me twenty-five cents and bought a dozen cookies for forty cents to take back to Helen. When I offered a cookie to the British students, they said, "You are just like all Americans; you throw your money around. It would give us indigestion to eat such expensive cookies." It occurred to me that someone bought their cookies when I was not there; they were baked for somebody. However, I did learn from them.

In November, both good and bad news arrived from America. The bad news was that the men's dormitory at SBI in Waxahachie, Texas, burned to the ground, and the school year was not half over. They had started re-building already. The good news was from Don Mallough, national secretary of the youth department at missions headquarters in Missouri. He said the New Mexico District youth president, Glen Anderson, had agreed for their state youth program to pay for a car and freight for us in Africa. We would pay the customs. The young people in the churches of New Mexico had car washes and multiple projects to raise money to provide vehicles for missionaries around the world. People of all ages got involved with a person's call. Reverend Mallough said we must send pictures and comments about the usefulness of the vehicle to him and Reverend Anderson when it arrived. We were very excited.

When it happened that Helen and I had two nights off at the same time, we visited the Bolton family at Ipswitch, on the coast east of London. The village was beautiful, and their house was lovely. Mr. Bolton's brother had married an American girl in China, and eventually they made their home in Helen's hometown in Pennsylvania. Our Bolton hosts took us on a drive up the coast of the North Sea. Since Ipswitch was just across the water from the continent of Europe, the first bomb in 1939 was dropped on a house just a block from the Boltons' home. We slept overnight in their son's room. To our surprise, the calendar on the wall was from Ellis Texaco

Service, East Central Avenue, Albuquerque, New Mexico. His auntie had sent it to him as they were touring the States. The world was getting smaller. The Boltons sold new and used cars with an adjacent bicycle and motorcycle shop. We bought our Raleigh bicycles from them for fifty dollars to take to Africa. We could leave them in Ipswitch until we needed them later. The money for mine came from SBI.

The British didn't get too excited about whether the pilgrims and Indians ate or starved, fought or made peace, so Helen and I went out to eat Thanksgiving dinner. We spent the next day at the Assembly of God Bible School in Kinley, Surrey County. We had coffee with Reverend Donald Gee, president, and he autographed a special book for each of us. I had read many of his books and even sold some at the bookstore at SBI. We borrowed a guitar and sang "I've Got A Mansion" in their evening chapel assembly. The students seemed delighted. Some of them were preparing to be missionaries. Finally, we went to visit the mothers and babies of our first deliveries; they were very special.

On another outing, we went to a cinema in London that showed only Christian movies. We had previously seen *I Beheld His Glory, The Robe,* and *The Ten Commandments.* When we saw Billy Graham's *Mr. Texas* (filmed in Fort Worth), feelings of nostalgia almost overwhelmed me. Since I had graduated from high school in Fort Worth, I imagined that I could smell those stockyards right in that London cinema. Other things had made me homesick, too. Mae and Dave were expecting my nephew David. Calvin and Evelyn were excited with the prospects of their first child (my first niece), Roxanne. Lois and Cecil Holley were planning for Ladean's arrival. Lola and Doyle Wilson were expecting Sharon—on and on. I thought, "Hey! I should go to America and set up a maternity home!" America was not ready for that in 1954.

It took all my spare time in the first week of December to address Christmas cards and add notes to them. It seemed so early that I was hardly in the Christmas spirit. Nevertheless, on a trip into London Helen bought me a posh English tea set for Christmas. I got her a souvenir compact and a leather portfolio for correspondence. Somehow, we must have gotten too tired as Helen took a horrible cold, and I had what they diagnosed as bursitis in my shoulders, so I missed some clinical practice. We were under considerable stress as we had heard that more than half of the previous class of pupil midwives had failed an important test at the end of this three-month rotation. If either of us failed a final exam, it would keep us both in England for an extra three months, as the mission board had said we were to stay together. One day in class, we were taught that if a complicated delivery occurred, a midwife must call a doctor in for consultation. Helen wrote me a note, "In Africa, you can call me, and I will call you." We had laughed a lot since the day we met. We laughed about things that happened on itinerary in America and then in England. It helped us relax. Practicing guitar and accordion together also helped. Near Christmas, Matron Lambert prepared a holiday meal for us since we were so far from home. Her specialty was a luscious, tasty trifle for desert. When she asked us how we liked it, Helen said, "Great, I was just thinking of asking for a trifle more." Matron said, "Well, that isn't nice!" and did not take it as a joke, the way the word is used in America. About a week before Christmas, we put up a small tree. We strung popcorn to decorate it. Miniature toys hung all over it. As our cards and gifts arrived from family and friends in America, we put them under the tree. In a package to Helen, her sister Mary and Mom Kopp included bedroom slippers and pajamas for me. A box came from Aunt Irene and Mamaw Layman in TorC. My sister and her family sent a Western Union greeting from San Diego. In a letter, Mae wrote, "Dave was transferred back to California from where you visited us in Virginia. Mom and Dad will be with us in San Diego for Christmas." Mr. and Mrs. Sternberg, from the Fair Store in Belen, wrote me a nice long letter. We were so blessed that I felt guilty. The African prayer group from SBI sent me fifteen dollars. I felt like sending it back since the boys' dorm had burned and I knew their students had so little money.

On Christmas Eve, Helen went caroling with a group of our classmates and to communion at the Church of England. I did not go; my back and shoulders were still bad. When they returned, we took pictures of our tree as we opened our gifts while our classmates helped us enjoy Christmas from America. You talk about a feast for Christmas Day! We ate chili with beans. We popped corn and took it on duty with us. The nurses seemed to enjoy it; they had never seen popcorn or pecans before. We walked through the wards to see how their decorations differed from America's. For one thing, we learned about Christmas firecrackers; they eventually became available in America. On New Year's Eve, we got off work late in the evening and attended a watch night service and banquet at a church across London from 10:00 P.M. until after midnight. A U.S. sailor was there—a sight for sore eyes! London public transportation discontinued at midnight, except the tubes. We had not asked about that! The cold still bothered me, and I had not put on enough clothing to keep out the damp wind. We walked for over two hours to Coniston Lodge on Tyrwhitt Road, spent the night, and slept until noon.

Finally, all the celebrations were over; we were left with almost two months of classes, clinical practice, and swatting the books seriously for an important state exam. I missed a week of the clinical experience because of my back and the bursitis, so I stayed at Redhill to make up clinical hours. Helen went home as a houseguest with P.M. Marjorie Edwards to Birmingham, an industrial town northwest of London. She said that she learned a lot. She told me about the guzunder under the bed as a nighttime bathroom and about a galvanized tub in the middle of the kitchen floor where they bathed on Saturday nights. Both of us had done that in childhood in the USA.

On February 9, Helen returned to London, where we met at Coniston Lodge and rented a room. We had little time for anything except for swatting the books for the next day. On February 10, at Russel Square in London, we took the first half of the state examination for midwifery. The written part took three hours. To relax after the exam, we went to see Billy Graham's *Oil Town U.S.A.* I made a visit to a doctor so I could be ready for the second half of midwifery training. At a physician's surgery, it took thirty minutes for the paper work, thirty minutes for them to explain why I should have gone to another doctor in the system, and three minutes to write me a prescription for pain in the back and shoulders. I was glad that America did not need government-run medicine.

At Coniston Lodge, we fed shillings, worth about a quarter, into the slot of an electric stove to stay warm enough to swat the books for the State oral exams on February 19. At zero-countdown we were introduced to a maternity patient whom we had never met. We were to calculate her due date, evaluate the possibility of twins or more, measure for bony pelvic adequacy, and discover toxemia or other abnormalities in her health profile. All this must be within the allotted time. Our findings were compared to the information placed on her chart earlier by her doctor. Then, the frantic waiting for results followed. That evening, Helen and I went to an all-night prayer meeting in the basement of Spurgeon's burned-out Tabernacle at Elephant and Castle.

While we were still at Coniston Lodge, Missionaries Floyd and Grace Thomas and their three daughters, Diana, Ruth, and Judi, arrived from California. Grace was a sister to Everett Smith at South Valley Assembly in Albuquerque, New Mexico. They were also staying at Coniston Lodge before going to the Gold Coast, the same country where we were going. We knew how to see London fast via the tubes, and it was cheaper, so we toured with them. We visited the British Press, equivalent to the Gospel Publishing House in the USA. At Westminster Abbey, we saw a plaque on the floor above where David Livingston's body was placed when it was retrieved from Africa. At St. Paul's Cathedral, we were shown the damage done by a missile during the blitz. What a waste! Helen brushed the dust from a statue of George Washington. At the Imperial War Museum we saw an unexploded guided missile. The Germans thrust these missiles at the British Isles, sometimes twenty-four hours a day, for six years. It amazed me that any people or buildings survived at all. I was so impressed that I hoped the world did not forget! One missile hit a Woolworth's store full of people. This was why America eventually agreed to help the British; it was part of WWII. The results of our exams arrived by post before the Thomas family left. Helen and I had passed the written and oral parts of this first half of our british midwifery training. The Thomases could personally deliver the good news of our success to mission officials in the Gold Coast. When they went on their way to Africa, it was like family leaving. We said, "See you in the Gold Coast in about eight months."

Sunday morning, February 28, in church at Buckingham Gate Westminster Chapel, Grady Wilson, Cliff Barrows, and Paul Mickelson of the Billy Graham team sat in front of us. They were in London for a crusade. On Sunday afternoon, we moved into a dormitory room in South London Hospital for Women and Children at Clapham Common, in London, S.W.4. We would be there three months. The rooms were heated, and the beds were better than any prior ones. My back improved. Next morning, we reported for duty about five blocks up the road at Queen Elizabeth Maternity Home. We passed a street called Nightingale Lane to get there. We would now be delivering babies on our own, with assistance available only if necessary. We were required to write up six cases, but I actually delivered twenty-seven babies in the three months. To learn how midwifery fit into the British medical system, we were also required to attend a series of lectures at the Royal College of Midwifery. This meant trips into London Town on the subway. Since we were walking the ten blocks round trip back to the hospital from QE for classes, we wrote Helen's Bolton friends at Ipswitch to send our three-speed Raleigh bicycles. When they first arrived, I got winded easily, so pushed my bike partway; that soon changed, and I was flying. The tables where we ate our meals at the QEMH stood on a platform; we asked about it. We were told, "An old man once had a Bible school here; this room was his chapel. His name was Spurgeon." I'm sure God has a sense of humor; the building was still being used to prepare recruits for missions!

In March, April, and May, the same three months we were delivering babies at QEMH, Billy Graham was in London for a crusade. At his Albuquerque Crusade a year prior, I was a nurse on duty. This time, Helen and I had certificates to sing in the choir. We attended his London Crusade about twice a week. There was an entrance to the subway right across the street from our hospital, so we and other pupil midwives could easily get to Harringay Arena. Roy Rogers and his wife, Dale Evans, gave their Christian testimony. Nostalgia made me tempted to return to California with them. At first, the news reports of Billy Graham were negative. As the crusade progressed, they became more objective. Finally, in one commentary, the reporter said he went forward and accepted Christ. The arena seated eleven thousand, and there were TV extension services at other locations. Saturday evening services were held in Wimbley Stadium, where about forty thousand attended. Sundays were left for the people to go to their own churches. The final Saturday night in May was described by Robert Glenton in the Sunday Express, ". . . 125,000 people were in Wembley Stadium the last night . . . a quarter again as many as that most famous first Wimbley Cup Final for tennis. With full motor coaches from Cardiff and Newcastle . . . ten microphones in front of him . . . the gaitered archbishop of Canterbury and the lord mayor of London sitting behind him, this . . . young American hushed the enormous crowd." "When Graham appealed for converts it was almost frightening. The walls of humanity started to break, first in a trickle, then in a rapidly moving stream—adding about 12,000 to their list—already nearing 33,000." Graham ended by saying, "Let's make tomorrow the greatest day your churches have ever known." After the last meeting at Wembley, we pupil midwives got on a big, red, double-decker, London bus to the nearest subway station. The bus driver was singing "Since Jesus Came into My Heart," along with his passengers. In the subway, men or women punching our tickets were singing "To God Be the Glory," and we joined in. As the trains sped through the tubes a commuter started singing, "Just As I Am" and it seemed all passengers joined in. It happened in the hospitals or other work places. Some pupil midwives said they went forward and accepted Christ during the three months. The impact it had on London is stamped on my mind forever.

For my birthday in May 1954, Helen bought me a cake and a dainty, Irish linen luncheon set, which I still prize. A Happy Birthday cable came from Mom and Dad. I dreamed that night that I flew home; two carloads of the family met me. In the morning, I felt that I had experienced a personal visit. The British celebrate Mother's Day in March, so I bought Mom a beautiful card and sent it closer to May. We were feeling quite at home in England, more so when we received a report of the total income tax and *superannuation* contributions (Social Security) withheld that year. I don't remember getting it back when we went to Africa.

Queen Elizabeth II, The Duke of Edinburgh, Prince Charles, and Princess Ann returned to London from a world tour in May. Helen and I saw them as they came ashore and entered their horsedrawn coach. It seemed all London was there—a crush of humanity. A story circulated about Prince

Charles. He was observing a man using a jackhammer to break up pavement. He got so close that the laborer said, "Be off with you!" That evening at play, the royal tot used audio to mock the laborer and jackhammer. His royal father insisted on an explanation, but his son ignored him. Finally, when his father came closer to demand a reply, Prince Charles looked up at his dad and said, "Be off with you!" There were different versions of the royal punishment.

For the last three months in London, we moved into the district house behind the hospital. Our clinical practice consisted of delivering babies, night or day, in the homes throughout the Brixton District of London. We soon understood the Cockney dialect very well. We had our own caseload of maternity clients. By then, I could ride my cycle up and down Tulse Hill and around Brixton without getting winded. Midwives were so respected that we were never afraid. We walked on a path through Matron Mudge's gorgeous flower garden from our residence to the hospital for classes. Her hydrangeas were mammoth. She took first place for her prize-winning garden in a competition by the Worshipful Company of Gardeners for the Best Hospital Garden in Metropolitan London.

Her garden made me think of the roses I had looked for so long ago. I could not know at the time, but that mystery would be solved years later in 1984 when my cousin Barbara Spencer Foster planned and directed our family reunion in Mountainair, New Mexico. I walked just across the street to the three-cornered house where I was born. It had evolved into a two-story house. I took a picture, then looked to my right. No roses and no trellis! I turned totally around to leave. Quite by accident, I looked to my right again and there they were, after sixty years! About a block away by the side of a new mortuary was an ancient house with a trellis. Now I knew that at age almost three, I had seen the roses "to my right" as we came off the porch and not when we walked to the porth hidden by tumble weeds!

I walked over to those dead rose vines and took pictures; a lifetime of mystery was solved! Rex and Lola Harris eventually tore down that old house and trellis of dry vines to enlarge the Harris-Hanlon Mortuary, but not until I found the roses!

We received our sailing date—September 19, 1954. We would go to Amsterdam and join a Holland West Africa Liner to the Gold Coast. In the meantime, back to reality. Before I could pedal over the hot sands of Africa, we must pedal over the hills of Brixton and deliver our quota of babies. There was also a quota of gas and air we must administer for analgesia. The gas and air equipment was brought to us when we phoned to say labor was well established. We had already met our maternity clients at prenatal clinics and some of their husbands at the Lamaze relaxation classes we were required to teach. The husband was usually in the home to help us. We could call for help in an emergency, and it arrived quickly. A grandmum was usually there to make the tea. The new mum must have a hot cup of tea ASAP after delivery, whether at home or hospital. We were experiencing, "Hurry up and wait." We swatted the books at the district house while waiting for the phone to ring. When it rang, we grabbed a map and rushed out to beat the stork to the address. It rained the whole month of June, so on each trip we got soaked, shoes and all. The eleventh baby delivered on my district rotation was a very important baby. Burt and Shelia Dalton were like many other young people; World War II had hindered them from having a family until a bit later. On July 21, 1954, the phone rang; I rushed up Tulse Hill on my cycle, and together we welcomed Jane. Shelia's parents were there; her mom made tea. Shelia showed me a special dress friends had custom-made for Jane. I ordered one in case my sister, Mae, or brother, Calvin, had a girl. My niece, Roxanne, got the dress.

The British Father's Day is in winter, but Dad's birthday and the American Father's Day is in June, so I sent him a

handkerchief and tie along with a humorous card. Dad
wrote thanks for the birthday thoughts and said my youngest brother was home from the navy; he had been in Korea.
On a birthday card to my mom in July, Helen wrote, "The
hankie is a little token of love to my western mom. We are
finishing up work on the district and studying for the coming second half of the midwifery state exam. . . . counting
on you and Pop Spencer to pray us through to flying colors.
We will be thinking of you folk when we board the Dutch
ship, Nigerstroom, at Amsterdam on the nineteenth of September. We have been told that we will be stationed at Sa-
boba Clinic, as we had hoped. Write often when we are in
Africa. Lots of love, Helen."

We got special permission to be off duty at the same time
on July 30. It was to celebrate our one-year anniversary of
being in England. At the American Embassy at Grosvenor
Square, we applied for our visas to the Gold Coast. A huge
statue of Franklin D. Roosevelt stood in Grosvenor Square.
We ate a lunch of real meat in a posh hotel down in London
Town. In August, I wrote home, "Once again we are packing
our suitcases, even as we go to final classes in midwifery.
We have been getting shots, visas for Africa, and tickets to
Holland and Africa. Our address in Holland would be: c/o
S. S. *Nigerstroom*, Holland West Afrika Lijn, N.V., Afrikahuis,
Spui 10-A, Amsterdam. Today, Monday, I rode my bike and
delivered my last baby as a pupil midwife." On Tuesday, we
had our bicycles crated, and we moved away from school
into a local bed-and-breakfast, as we were students no more.
We started swatting for the final exams we must take before
sailing.

On Friday, September 3, our nine-day Cooks Tour started. Helen and I were determined to relax before our exams
and not get under stress by entertaining a thought of either
failing. We claimed Matthew 18:19 as our strength. We chose
the long seat in the rear of the bus so we could study and not
disturb others. On the first day, we sent postcards to fam-

ily and friends in America from Oxford University and its forty colleges and from Shakespeare country on the Avon River. Of all the great cathedrals we visited, I was more in awe of Litchfield and York Minster. Some buildings were dated 1492. We went through villages where roofs on homes were thatched. Some houses had settled crookedly. I took a picture of a cat looking out one crooked window and half expected to see a crooked little man, mouse, or dog walk out the crooked door! In Scotland, we drove through heather meadows and saw sheep of different colors feeding. Our guide told us that they were the sheep raised to weave the tartan plaid. Even when he admitted it was really to dip them for ticks, I wondered why the different colors. Perhaps the dip color was dated; just by looking at group of sheep they knew the date of dipping.

At the Palace of Holyrood House in Edinburgh, the flag was flying, so that meant Queen Elizabeth II was in residence at the time. Because of that, our visit was limited to certain rooms in the palace. While we did not go across to the northernmost parts of Scotland, we were taken to the Forth Bridge, which spans the water just before it widens eastward into the Firth of Forth. A crew has been painting that bridge since the day it opened in 1890, about the year my grandfather arrived in the Manzano Mountains of New Mexico! Glasgow was an industrial city, like London. Smoggy! We did not even spend the night there; we were due in London. The twenty-three sightseers were mostly Americans from eight different states.

⁓

Helen and I were about to face even a tighter schedule than kept on the tour. By Sunday, September 12, we were back in our London bed and breakfast. On Monday, we went to the school, where our mail was being held. A letter said my niece, Roxanne, had been born August 25. I went to where our freight was stored, dug through it and found the dress for her. I mailed it to the USA, along with my recent Scottish plaid purchases. We shipped our freight to a steamer on the east coast of England with only a day left for rest and swatting the books. On Wednesday, in London, we sat for the second exam of the central midwives board. At one point, I sat across from a doctor, an anesthesiologist, and a matron. Questions about pathology, analgesia, and midwifery were asked in rapid fire, for ten minutes. One question was, "How will you know when a black woman is cyanotic?" I replied, "I will have opportunity to observe normal skin color and will note changes."

On Thursday, September 16, we rushed to the hospital to get our mail. We had both passed the exam! Another letter said our ship was sailing a day early, so we had to get to the east coast and join our freight. This forced us to phone our families in America one day earlier than scheduled; Mom, Dad, and Royce were surprised. Calvin had planned to drive from Albuquerque to Belen on the date scheduled, so he missed my call. We did not say much, but I felt that I had a visit. Later, we cried a little. That same day, we took a train to the east coast where an overnight sleeper took us across the North Sea to The Hague, Netherlands. It was no sleeper! The sea was so rough that we were kept awake and hanging onto our bunks, but we were only slightly seasick. A train ride from The Hague to Amsterdam let us see the windmills of Holland and the neat, clean countryside. The people were friendly, and many spoke English. It seemed that Continental Europeans felt the need to speak English. We had observed that many of the British people spoke French or some European Continental language. A cablegram from Mom and Dad was waiting at the small hotel where we spent the night. We had kept the captain of the M.S./S.S. *Nigerstroom* informed of our lodging place in Amsterdam. Things were happening quickly. Only one day remained for us to tour Amsterdam via canals.

We joined our ship for Africa on Saturday, September 18.

The rooms were large with private baths. The ship began to move near midnight. It took the rest of the night to go from Amsterdam through the locks to the North Sea. In going through the locks, the walls seemed so close on each side that my claustrophobia kicked in and never allowed sleep. The odor of diesel sent into our rooms made the air seem heavy and hard to breathe. It was a long night and morning was welcome. Most passengers were a bit nauseous from the locks and now the rough North Sea. We learned that there were twenty-four passengers aboard, less than the one hundred on the *Veendam* from USA to England. Going south and a bit west, we passed the Hook of Holland, Flanders, and went along the Strait between England and France. One of the nine missionaries aboard was leading devotions when we glided past the white cliffs of Dover. Some passengers were Americans, but none were from our church denomination. At the far west point of France, we turned back southeast into the Bay of Biscay. It was rougher, and we were more seasick. The captain said we should eat something before we got out of bed each morning; it might decrease the nausea. Next morning, I reached for the bread that I had placed beside my bed and ate some. My diary says, "I handed Helen a piece, and she did eat." When we turned on a light to dress, we saw the sack containing the bread was covered with ants. That gave us another reason to be nauseated. The M.V. *Nigerstroom* moved slowly into the Bay of Gironde, the graveyard. Parts of hulls and spars from WWII were protruding, all askew, out of the water in a long row. It seemed as if they had been swept to the middle with a broom to clear the channel for ships to pass on either side. The sight made me ask, "What about the men on those ships?"

Our ship docked at Bordeaux, France. We had difficulty finding anyone to speak English. We got seventeen hundred francs for five dollars. We bought stamps, mailed twenty-two letters, and discovered delicious Bordeaux pickles. In the basement of St. Michael's Cathedral with a tour group, we saw mummified bodies in an upright position all around the walls. As nurses, we tried to decide what caused each death. We left Bordeau on September 23 and immediately became seasick again. As Helen put it nicely, "We emptied our tummies." We were never very far from land as we passed Spain and Portugal. By the time we could see the Rock in the distance and passed the Strait of Gibralter, we were sick of the sea! The *Nigerstroom* moved out into calmer seas and turned straight south through the Spanish Canary Islands off the west coast of Morocco. Africa was so near; the weather was getting warmer. A school of flying fish, family Exocoetidae, was playing alongside the ship. One landed on the deck, and a crewmember spread its wing-fins for us to see.

On Thursday, August 30, we awoke to discover the ship was docked at Dakar, the westernmost point of Africa. We were allowed off ship from 4:00 to 8:00 P.M. There, in Senegal, we first set foot on African soil! In a market, we bought gum, shampoo, and tatting thread. The ship went to sea that night as we slept. Next morning, I led devotions, using I Timothy 2:1–6.

That day, the anchor was dropped into deep water near Freetown, Sierra Leone. About fifty African men came aboard; they unloaded and loaded freight all night long. Two dived from the edge of the ship for coins thrown into the Atlantic. Our ship left Freetown after we went to sleep. Sometime in the night, I awoke with dysentery. At breakfast we discovered that the ship's officers, crew, and passengers had done the same, all except a woman everyone knew drank alcohol freely—and Helen. She got teased about why this missionary and the lush were the only two not having the problem! When the ship docked at Monrovia, Liberia, on October 5, a doctor came aboard and distributed Terramycin. We were told that the ship's cook was guilty of spreading the offending bacteria. Helen and I decided to visit the Assemblies of God Mission in Monrovia town. A lorry (truck) stopped, and we boarded it. The owner could see we were two excited novices and charged us two dollars to ride into town. The American dollar was their currency. The resident missionaries, the W. J. Kornelsens, were in America on furlough, but an older couple was house sitting. They said two dollars was too much to pay for fare from the harbor. Going back to the ship we paid the driver twenty-five cents. As the Africans say, "And did you learn anything?" Our education had started! I found this little item in a 1950 Pentecostal Evangel. It said, "Missionaries leaving Springfield on January 17 for Africa, aboard the mission-owned plane, *Ambassador II*, were Mr. and Mrs. W. J. Kornelsen, Liberia, and Mr. and Mrs. George Anderson, Gold Coast. Henry B. Garlock, field secretary for Africa, also was a passenger to Africa." We were there in 1954, so the Kornelsens and Andersons were truly due for a furlough!

The next stop was Abidjan, Ivory Coast, where we took a two-hour walk. The buildings and flora were tropical, similar to Southern California and Arizona. The people were friendly, but spoke only French and African dialects. We were pleasantly tired and ready for a good night's sleep when we got back to the ship. Tomorrow we would arrive at the Gold Coast, the West African County we had prepared for; it had taken years!

# Appendix

THIS PLAY IS PRESENTED in loving memory of Mabel Ruth Wallace, who influenced me to become a Christian. She was a sister to Annelle (Wallace) Burroughs and Elsie (Pendleton) Carl; it may be useful.

## A Heavenly Call

By: MRW & ECS, 1939.

*Present this play and it will pay for buying my book!*

Written in 1939 by Mabel Ruth Wallace and Elsie Charlese Spencer, ages fifteen years. This handwritten play was sent to me from Annelle, Mabel's younger sister, in 1994. She had received it from their mother, Etta Wallace, before she died.

| Main Characters | Ages | Shadow Characters |
|---|---|---|
| Stanley Harrington | 19 years | Mrs. Smith |
| Sibyl Gaylord | 18 years | Children (2 or 3) |
| Sue Gaylord | 13 years | "S. B. "Somebody" |
| Melvyn Gaylord | 16 years | Su Ching |
| Grandma Gaylord | 70 years | Paul, a U.S.A. co-worker |
| Ann Pendleton | 15 years | A Native |

Time beginning: In January.
Ends: A year later at Christmas
Setting (Of Act I and III): A living room
Setting (Act II): Inside of hut in China

## Act I

Time: January.
Setting: In a Living Room.

(Ann and Sue enter laughing and remove wraps. Melvyn enter directly behind. They have been on a sleigh ride. Grandma Gaylord is already seated in the room by the fire.)

Ann (Seating herself during speech): It's too bad Stanley is leaving just when our winter sports are beginning.

Sue (Seating herself): Not too bad! Remember the Lord is sending him.

Melvyn (Crossing room and slumping down in a chair): Wheee! it's really cold out there.

Ann (Jokingly and turning to him): It wouldn't do for you to go to China. You'd freeze.

Melvyn (Lazily): Yes? I don't see you going.

Grandma: Missionaries don't usually think of the weather; they think of lost souls. (A knock at the door.)

Sue (Going to door): I'll get it. (Mrs. Smith enters.)

Mrs. Smith: Hello, everybody. (Apron on, starts for kitchen after her wraps are removed.)

Sue (Busying herself): We must hurry and fix the hot chocolate and sandwiches before the crowd comes.

Ann (Starting for kitchen): Let me help. (A Pause)

Melvyn: We're really going to miss Stan in our Young People's services.

Sue: Maybe the Chinese need him more than we do, but Sibyl will probably be the one who will miss him most. (Goes to window and looks out, then returns to chair) Wonder why they haven't come? (Knock at the door. Sue goes to the door. Two or three children enter.)

Sue: My! You look like winter itself. Better warm yourselves!

One Child: Where's Stanley and Sibyl?

Sue: They should be here soon.

Any child: Have you seen Frank's new accordion, Melvyn?

Melvyn: (Waves hand as if uninterested.) No, but that's an idea. Why doesn't someone get a guitar and let's sing? Sue, you get it.

S.B.: Let's sing "The Final Payday." (They sing.) (Stanley and Sibyl enter. Everybody greets noisily.)

Stanley: Go ahead and sing. That sounds good.

Sue: How about you two singing a duet?

S.B.: Sing "I Won't Have To Cross Jordan Alone."

Sibyl: (Turning) Shall we?

Stanley: Suits me. (They sing.) (Ann enters while they sing and Sue leaves to help Mrs. Smith bring in refreshments. All get quiet, look at Stanley. He "returns thanks" to God for the food. The crowd talks as they eat.)

Sue: Shhh! Everyone think of a scripture to quote and we'll have a Scripture shower when we've finished eating.

Melvyn: Ummm, I'm not so good at that.

Ann: Well, if you're not, you better read your Bible more.

We all need to. (Scripture shower proceeds.)

Sibyl: Stanley, why don't you tell us about your calling to China? I'm sure everyone's interested.

Stanley: (Standing) Well, I hardly know how to begin, but the first time the Lord spoke to me, I was about twelve years old. I had been saved only a short time. I saw a vision. I saw, in China, fields of rice ready for the harvesters. As I looked on, the fields gradually turned into people. Then I found myself in the midst of them preaching the Word of God. My heart has been burdened, ever since, for the work in China. (He raises one shoulder and spreads his hands as he says the last line and sits.)

Grandma: It's 10:20.

Sue: Shall we pray? It will soon be time for Stanley to leave. (Sue, Ann and one other person prays.)

Grandma: It's 10:30 and your train leaves soon enough, so I guess you'd better hurry unless you want to get left. (Everybody says good-bye to Stanley. Some shake hands, some wave as he leaves the room.)
(Curtain.) (End of First Act)

## Act II

Time: November, a year later.
Setting: Inside of hut in China. (Stanley is sitting in a chair reading the Bible. A knock is heard, and he goes to the door. Su Ching enters.)

Stanley: How do you do, Su Ching?

Su Ching: (With a Chinese accent.) Brother Harrington, here's a list of names who want to enroll in our Mission School. We will need another teacher.

Stanley: Really? But that's impossible. I got a letter from the mission board saying there is no one available. I've been praying for the Lord to send someone to help us. We'll just have to trust Him. How is Sister Tu Wung? I hope she is better.

Su Ching: Yes, she's better. She's been helping get names for the mission school.

Stanley: Praise the Lord!

Su Ching: I have to go now.

Stanley: Shall we pray before you go? Let's pray especially for God to send another teacher. (They pray.)

Su Ching: Good-bye, Brother Harrington. God bless you!

Stanley: Come again, Su Ching, and continue to pray for a teacher. (Su Ching leaves and Stanley reads Bible again.) (Another knock and Brother Paul enters.)

Stanley: Hello, Paul. Did you have a safe trip?

Paul: Yes, we did. We were not attacked at all and we saw no signs of trouble. We had a good meeting. Eleven said they accepted Christ; seven were baptized.

Stanley: Good! Su Ching came today with the list of those enrolled in our mission school; nearly eight hundred! We must have another teacher. We are praying for one. I don't know— (A knock at the door. Stanley goes to the door. A Native enters.)

Native: Letters for you, Brother Harrington. (Stanley nods head and the Native leaves.)

Stanley: (Looking at the letters.) Mind if I read my mail?

Paul: Go right ahead. (Stanley reads silently. Then suddenly flings up his hands.)

Stanley: Praise the Lord! God has answered our prayers already. Listen to this: "I have felt a definite call for the—" (Stanley looks up.) This is from Sibyl. "I have felt a definite call for the work in China. I am arranging with the mission board to return with you as you go back from your Christmas vacation." (Stanley looks at Paul.) Isn't that grand? Praise the Lord.

Paul: But who's Sibyl?

Stanley: Haven't I told you before? She's a dear friend of mine at home, a very fine Christian girl. She'll be just the one for the new teacher! I think I'll go pack. Christmas is coming. (He jumps up enthusiastically.) (Curtain)

## Act III

Time: Christmas.
Setting: Living room at Stanley's home.

Grandma: "I wonder why those children don't come. They should have been here thirty minutes ago."

Mrs. Smith: I have supper ready for them. Don't worry.

Grandma: They'll probably be really hungry. It will be nice having Stanley back for awhile, but taking Sibyl back with him is going to make it lonesome for us.

Mrs. Smith: Yes, because Sibyl is such a dear and ever so good as a worker. (She goes to the window and looks out.) I guess they decided to take a ride before coming home. (Pause) Stanley has already done a great work in China, hasn't he?

Grandma: Yes, and he needs help. (Enter: Stanley, Sibyl and Melvyn, and Sue.)

Stanley: Hello, Grandma! Mrs. Smith! It's really cold in this country, but I'm mighty glad to be here! (He shakes hands with both.)

Melvyn: Stanley's some preacher. He talked all the way home. Looks like Sibyl will have to go some to keep up with him.

Sibyl: I should say so! The Lord will have to help me. I won't have all of *you* around to help me.

Stanley: Oh, but we'll have good friends there, very capable, dear and faithful workers. You will have help, Sibyl.

Sue: (Looking toward dining room.) We'd better go eat and get ready or we'll be late to our Christmas program.

Melvyn: Let's go. (All scramble through a door, except Grandma and Mrs. Smith, who straggle behind.)

Grandma: That is truly a dear group of children. It makes me happy, yet I'm sorry to think they are leaving again so soon. The Lord is the best one for us to give them to. He will protect them and guard them better than we can.

Mrs. Smith: Exactly. Thank God, He can. (She stretches her hand toward the kitchen.) The food is there, I must go home and dress for the Christmas program.

Grandma: Thank you. Good-bye. Grandma goes through the door where the others went. Mrs. Smith exits an opposite door.)

(With curtains closed, the Announcer steps to center stage)

Announcer: One week has passed. (He leaves.)

(Curtains open with Grandma sitting alone. Enter: Melvyn, Stanley, Sibyl and Sue.)

Melvyn: Sibyl, I'm mighty proud of you. Stanley, you better take good care of my big sis. Maybe when you come back again, I'll be a better boy. I'm beginning, even now, to feel a little mean. You may pray for me once in a while if you still want to.

Sibyl: Thank the Lord for that! I have a wonderful little brother.

Stanley: Me, too. (Shrugs shoulders and chuckles.)

Sue: What about me? Am I good?

Sibyl: (Hugging Sue and laughing.) You're the dearest little sister on earth. Won't you pray for me a lot while I'm away? It'll be good to know you're remembering me.

Melvyn: Did you say your train leaves in less than two hours?

Stanley: Yes, and we must go so we'll be there on time. We must— What time is it? We must be going now. Are your things all ready, Sibyl?

Sibyl: Yes, I believe they are. (She kisses Grandma and Sue and shakes hands with Melvyn.) Good-bye, dear ones. Always remember me in prayer.

Stanley: (Waving hand.) Good-bye. Pray for the school and all our work in China. Good-bye.(As the curtain closes slowly.)

Grandma: (With a sly smile.) Yeah, and we'll be waiting for that beautiful, big wedding when you come on your next leave.

Melvyn and Sue together: (Seen laughing, walking toward Grandma and waving their hands.) Ahh, Grandma.

(The End)

# About the Author

PERHAPS ONLY AN UNMARRIED person could have time for a degree, license, diploma or certificate in technology, banking, medical, clergy and education involving eleven institutions above the 4-year high school level. I have had hands-on experience in all these and taught in some. Mail arrives from around the world to Rev., Prof., Dir., RN, Miss, (the diminishing) MS, CNM and SCM (England and Africa.). The Africans just say, "She is still our 'Madam.'" Read her book, *Welcome, Madam!* to learn how the Africans arrived at this respectful title they gave her.

# Reference List

Cheney, Lois A. 1969. *God Is No Fool.* Abington Press.

Thomas, Shirley. 1939. *Men of Space.* Philadelphia: Chilton Company Publishers.

*Yoakum County History:* Sponsored by the TSA MO GA Club in Plains, Texas. Special thanks to Wilma Powell and Mrs. P. W. St. Romain for their assistance.

*History of Ben Spencer* by various members of the Roy Spencer family (duplicated pages from 2003).

Printed in the United States
65238LVS00002B/1-99

9 781587 365539